Tea with the King

Tea with the King

40 Tea Time Devotions

Sue Erickson

Copyright © 2018 by Sue Erickson. All rights reserved.

No part of this publication may be reproduced in any form without the written permission of the author.

All scripture quotations, unless otherwise indicated, are taken from the New King James Version®. Copyright © 1982 by Thomas Nelson. Used by permission. All rights reserved.

Scripture quotations indicated as NIV are taken from the Holy Bible, New International Version ®, NIV®. Copyright © 1973, 1978, 1984, 2011 by Biblica, Inc.® Used by permission. All rights reserved worldwide.

Scripture quotations taken from the New American Standard Bible® (NASB), Copyright © 1960, 1962, 1963, 1968, 1971, 1972, 1973, 1975, 1977, 1995 by The Lockman Foundation
Used by permission. www.Lockman.org

Cover by Rebecca McCartney

ISBN-13: 978-1722441203
ISBN-10: 1722441208

Dedication

To my parents, Jean and Reno Belmessieri, who have supported me through the years in everything that has been important to me. I am so grateful for you.

Acknowledgements

First and foremost, I want to thank my Lord Jesus Christ for giving me the idea for this book and directing my words throughout its creation. He gave me the passion for tea and the passion for His Word without which there would be no book. Thank You, Lord.

My heartfelt thanks and gratitude for the ladies of The Write Bunch. I am so grateful for your patience as you listened to me read these devotions. I thank you for your gentle criticism and wonderful encouragement!

My thanks and appreciation to my niece, Michelle Belmessieri, who graciously edited my work and made sure all my commas and dashes were in the right place. Thank you.

Last but not least, thanks to my sister, Debbie Belmessieri, who helped me with the cover text. I appreciate all of your encouragement.

You are all the best. I lift my tea cup to all of you!

Contents

You Are Invited To Tea ……………….......……………	11
Taking Tea with the King ………………………………..	13
If Teacups Could Talk …………………………………….	15
It's Always Tea Time! ……………………………………..	17
The Best Book of All ……………………………………..	21
What's In a Name? ……………………………………….	23
RSVP Required …………………………………………….	25
Chosen by God ……………………………………………	27
His Treasured Possession ………………………………..	29
Steeped in the Word …………………………………….	31
Instructions for Life ……………………………………...	33
Bread of Life ……………………………………………...	35
Who Are You, Really? …………………………………..	37
A Vessel for His Glory …………………………………..	39
Tea and Friendship ……………………………………...	41
Sharing Through Hospitality ……………………………	43
Cultivating Your Spiritual Garden ……………………...	45
His Footsteps, My Pathway …………………………….	47
He Who Has Ears to Hear ……………………………...	49
Ah, That Fragrant Aroma! ……………………………...	51
The Gift Giver …………………………………………...	53
The King of Glory ……………………………………….	55
Tea by the Sea …………………………………………..	57

Is Anybody Home?	61
Words of My Mouth	65
Engraved on the Palms of His Hands	67
The Everlasting Arms	69
Worth the Wait	71
Broken Before God	75
Lay That Burden Down	77
A Cup of Chaos	79
Soul Spa	83
Comfort in a Cup	85
Tea for Two	87
Let the Children Come	89
"Old" is a Good Thing	93
A Tea Hat or a Crown	95
Dressed for Heaven	97
Seated at His Table	99
What Will You Choose Today?	101
Are You Ready?	103
Notes	107

You Are Invited to Tea

The book you hold in your hands invites you in to enjoy the Word of God over a cup of tea. There is no greater joy than to savor His presence, to "taste and see that the Lord is good," to delve into His Word and know Him more fully.

My prayer is that you will find more of Him and know Him more deeply and intimately as you read these pages. Be sure to invite Him to join you over a cup of your favorite tea. Sit in the garden, on the beach, beside a stream in the woods, on a mountaintop, or in your favorite chair where your heart can be quiet and you can hear His voice.

Allow Him to fill you with His own words and remind you of how much He loves you and desires your company. Explore His precious and magnificent promises to you. He makes for a most wonderful companion at tea time.

Taking Tea with the King

Have you ever imagined yourself having tea with the Queen? Maybe you're in the Queen's favorite sitting room or at a tea table in the palace garden. You're being served from a silver tea service, enjoying delicious dainties, while discussing the latest exploits of the royal family.

Chances are you will never be invited to tea with the Queen. Her schedule is very full and her invitations only go out to a select few. If you're lucky enough to be invited, at the end of tea you will be dismissed. But you can do something even better…

You can take tea with the King!

Most of us desire more than a passing encounter with royalty. We want to be loved and cherished. We long for intimacy. We want to feel that we belong. Unlike earthly monarchs, our King is always available. His schedule is never full. He always has time for us and longs to be with us. He is just waiting for our invitation. And He will not dismiss us.

Who is this King? He is Jesus Christ, the King of Kings, the only Sovereign, the King of Glory. He is the God of all creation, including the tea leaves you are steeping.

So prepare a pot of your favorite tea, grab your Bible and your teacup, sit in your favorite chair, and invite the King to tea. You will not be disappointed.

"Come to Me, all you who labor and are heavy laden, and I will give you rest. Take My yoke upon you and learn from Me, for I am gentle and lowly in heart, and you will find rest for your souls. For My yoke is easy and My burden is light" (Matthew 11:28-30).

If Teacups Could Talk

Every teacup has its own story. If you are like me, each teacup in your collection may arouse memories of special occasions, places you've travelled, certain friends and loved ones, lovely tea parties, or even different cultures. If these cups could talk, the stories they could tell!

Many of my cups have made the long trip halfway around the world from China to my table. They could probably tell of life in a factory; of being tightly wrapped and closely packed for months in crates on a ship; of experiencing both calm and angry seas; of being moved from place to place before being displayed on a shelf in some shop; and of being chosen to come home and belong to me.

My beautiful hand painted Imperial Porcelain teacups from St. Petersburg, Russia, could tell us the history of the Czars of that nation; stories of the caravans that carried bold black teas across China on the backs of camels for their samovars; and of the talented hands that painted these beauties.

My great grandmother's dainty teacup rimmed with gold and soft pink roses could tell me about the woman I never met; about my grandmother's childhood home and family in San Francisco at the turn of the 20th century; of their family tea time traditions and what teas my great grandmother used to fill her teacup. I have so many questions that her teacup could answer if it could just speak.

If the teacups on my shelves could tell their stories, the chatter would be deafening, but extremely interesting. If the teapots joined in, there would be no end of entertainment! How I wish they could share their histories with me.

One of the things I love about the Bible are all the stories of the people who fill its pages – their strengths and weaknesses; their successes and failures; their relationships with others (both good and bad); the histories of the generations of their families; their culture and daily life; their stories of faith; and most of all, their encounters with

God and with our Lord Jesus. The Bible has so many stories to tell us if we take the time to explore its pages.

We each have a unique story to tell, too. No two lives are identical. We all have personalities, families, experiences, and paths through life that are unique and ordained by God just for us. Throughout Scripture, we are instructed to remember, especially those things that God has done for us. God's goodness to us is something to hold on to when life gets bumpy or challenging.

Psalm 77 is a song of remembrance of the redemptive works of God in David's life. David instructs Israel to "Remember His marvelous works which He has done" (1 Chronicles 16:12) and the psalmist assures God in Psalm 119:16, "I will not forget Your Word." Paul's final farewell to the church in Ephesus encouraged them to remember the words of the Lord Jesus (Acts 20:35). Timothy was told to "remember that Jesus Christ, of the seed of David, was raised from the dead" (2 Timothy 2:8). When we partake of communion, we are to eat and drink in remembrance of Jesus and what He did on the cross for us (1 Corinthians 11:23-26).

If we were to sit down and tell our life story, hopefully it would be filled with the evidence of God's goodness to us, made plain through the stories we tell as we remember His hand on our lives. My story would recount how He pursued me until there was nowhere I could go except to Him; of the years of loneliness and despair that culminated in meeting and falling in love with the Lord Jesus; how He opened a door to attend a year of Bible College when I was struggling with a career change; of the precious people He has brought into my life; of my family which He specifically chose for me; of trials and temptations and testing, all of which He has seen me through; of trips to different countries and new cultures; of joys, fond memories and opportunities to serve Him by serving others; and of seven years in the tea business which opened up a new world to me.

Of course, all of these stories would be told over a cup of tea! So, I will steep a pot of tea for us and let the stories begin.

It's Always Tea Time!

I've been thinking lately about the mystery we call "Time." Honestly, it is something I am not able to wrap my mind around. Just reading what Wikipedia has to say about it, my brain feels like it's about to explode. Webster defines time as "a continuous period measured by clocks, watches and calendars; the period or moment in which something takes place." It can be past, present and future, though it only moves forward. We measure it in seconds, minutes, hours, days, weeks, months and years. We measure it using various tools such as sundials, watches, clocks, calendars, and a host of modern scientific inventions. The ancient Greeks personified time as the gods Chronos (numerical time) and Kairos (opportune time). Philosophers such as Kant and Newton have tried to define time in philosophical terms. Scientists with familiar names like Einstein and Hawking have theorized about time, explaining it as relative, flexible or even an illusion. Psychologists have found that one's perception of time may be impaired by disease or altered with drugs. Do you understand why my mind is spinning?

I much prefer the Mad Hatter's commentary on time when he pronounces that "It's always tea time!" At the crazy tea party that Alice attends in Wonderland, the Mad Hatter speaks of time as a person rather than something that can be wasted. The March Hare takes out his watch and proceeds to dunk it into his tea because it isn't good for telling time anymore. It is stuck on six o'clock. That's why it is always tea time. Even the White Rabbit carries a pocket watch which he keeps a close eye on as he seems to always be running late to somewhere.

How is time defined in Scripture? It is something that God lives outside of and has total control over. It is a framework which He has created in which to place all of His creation. Past, present and future is all contained within time, and God dwells outside of time in what He calls Eternity (Isaiah 57:15a). I'm still having a hard time wrapping my mind around all of this. Thank goodness that God has it all under control.

In God's economy, everything has a time and a purpose. "To everything there is a season, and a time for every purpose under heaven…He has made everything beautiful in its time" (Ecclesiastes 3:1, 11). He has also put eternity in our hearts which drives us to try to understand what it is and how we fit into it, though I doubt we will ever fully comprehend it because God's ways are just too great for our finite minds. How can the finite understand the infinite? I think as long as we dwell within time, we will not grasp eternity until we step into it. Won't that be mind-boggling!

Do you remember as a child how agonizingly slow time could pass? Sometimes we thought it would never end. Now as an adult, I marvel at how quickly time passes by, increasingly fast, making me feel like I've been left spinning in the dust after a whirlwind. I find myself praying that the Lord will slow it down for me sometimes. Maybe time *is* relative depending upon our age. Yet with God, a thousand years in His sight are just like yesterday in ours (Psalm 90:4; 2 Peter 3:8). Though we are unable to know how many days and years we have been granted ahead of time, God knows the days of our lives. The Psalmist reminds us that our time on this earth is short and we will all see death at some point (Psalm 89:47-48).

One of my favorite verses are the wise words spoken by David: "My times are in Your hand" (Psalm 31:15a). I can trust that the days that are ordained for me are totally secure in God's hands. I wonder sometimes why God chose to give me life in the time and place I live in. Why this country? Why this century? Why this nationality? I don't need to know that, but rest in the fact that God knows what He is doing. Paul addressed this subject when he spoke before the citizens of Athens on one of his missionary journeys. "He has made from one blood every nation of men to dwell on all the face of the earth, and has determined their preappointed times and the boundaries of their dwellings" (Acts 17:26). God in His wisdom chose to give me life at this point in time, in my family, and in this country. It was all appointed for me before I came into existence.

As I sit here with my thoughts wandering all over the place, I rest in the fact that God has my days all under control and has placed me right where He wants me to be. I live within the confines of the time that He has created. One day soon, I will step into eternity to meet Him face to face. Until then, I will continue to seek Him out in His Word and sip my tea, because "It's always tea time."

The Best Book of All

Over the past few years I have compiled a small library of books about "everything tea." Children's books tell stories about taking tea and using proper etiquette. There are books about the history of tea, the health benefits of tea, famous people in the tea industry, tea travel, recipes for afternoon tea, tea-themed devotions and more. They instruct, inform, and delight me on a much-loved subject; however, they cannot change me or my character. But God's Word can.

Two winters ago, California was inundated with rain, ending a long period of severe drought. There were many areas around the Central Valley that experienced flooding. I've often thought if there was an impending disaster and I only had time to grab one book, it would be my Bible. What difference does this book make in my life? It is an anchor for me in a world filled with trouble. It is God's love letter to me. It instructs, informs, and delights me much more than my tea library.

Yet it goes much deeper than that. It changes me from the inside out. It convicts me of sin. It teaches, rebukes, corrects, and trains me in the righteousness of God so that I am equipped to do good works for Him (2 Timothy 3:16). This Word is living and active, sharper than a two-edged sword that pierces my soul and spirit; it judges my thoughts and the motivations of my heart (Hebrews 4:12). It is God's truth (John 17:17).

God's Word gives me life (Psalm 119:50) because "man does not live on bread alone but on every word that comes from the mouth of the Lord" (Deuteronomy 8:3b NIV). Jesus Himself said, "The words that I speak to you are spirit, and they are life" (John 6:63). Even the apostles recognized that only Jesus has words of eternal life (John 6:68). His Word is all I need so that I can know the Father, the Son, and the Holy Spirit.

How could I read this book and not be changed? If His Spirit is in me, Scripture will change me. And, oh, how I need to be changed to be made more like Him. Yes, when life's floods surround me, I am reaching for my Bible (and a cup of tea) to spend time with my King.

Father, please open my heart and mind to receive all You have for me today from Your Word. Use it to change me, to make me more like Jesus, to help me understand His ways, so I am equipped to do Your will today. Amen.

What's In a Name?

TEA is a three letter word. Such a small word for a leaf that has changed the world! Tea has influenced so many areas of life: high society and common laborers; espionage and smuggling; wars between nations; the rise and fall of many fortunes; spiritual quests; cultural ceremonies; health and well-being; and the list goes on. It's safe to say that the discovery and development of this leaf has changed the world.

TEA is a small word with many variations, but all represent the same leaf that makes the beverage we enjoy all over the world today. Tea in any language is derived from Chinese words "cha" or "tay." [1] Here are just a few examples:

    Thé – French   Cha – Japanese
    Té – Spanish   Chai – Russian/Hindi
    Tee – German   Shai – Arabic
    Thee – Dutch   Chá – Portuguese
    Te – Hebrew   Chay – Turkish

This small word packs quite a punch when we look at its impact on the world: its history; its varieties; its cultural impact globally; the tea industry from cultivation on tea plantations to blending, packaging and distribution; research; classes and seminars; conferences and trade shows – all from this single plant.

However, there is another three letter word with a greater impact, a life changing one: GOD. He is the creator of that tea plant! He also has many names found throughout the Bible that each depict a different aspect of His character. It is by the variety of His names that we can even begin to know in part who He is. It is worth examining further so we can know and appreciate who He is more deeply. Here are examples of only a few names, but so expressive of who He is in our lives when we surrender to Him.[2]

    Elohim – Creator (Deuteronomy 6:4)
    El Shaddai – Almighty God (Genesis 17:1)

Adonai – Lord (Genesis 15:2)

Jehovah – LORD, The Self-Existent One (Exodus 3:14-15)

Jehovah-jireh – The LORD will Provide (Genesis 22:1-19)

Jehovah-shalom – The LORD is Peace (Isaiah 9:6; 26:3; Philippians 4:6-9)

Jehovah-rapha – The LORD who Heals (Exodus 15:26; Psalm 147:3; 1 Peter 2:24)

Jehovah-raah – The LORD my Shepherd (Psalm 23:1; Isaiah 40:11; John 10:11)

There are so many more names for our God in Scripture. He is our Savior and Redeemer; Son of God and Son of Man; our Friend; the Lion and the Lamb; the Alpha and Omega; Author of our faith; our Righteousness; Lord—all these names reflecting the character of Jesus Christ, God's Son. One day, all the earth will recognize the One who is Creator and Lord, Jesus Christ. One day, at the sound of His Name, every knee will bow and every tongue will confess that Jesus is Lord (Philippians 2:9-11).

So, what's in a name? Everything! His Name is life to us who believe. "There is no other Name under heaven given among men by which we must be saved" (Acts 4:12). This Name changes us from the inside out. He is the lover of our souls and all we need to live.

"O LORD, we have waited for You; The desire of our soul is for Your Name and for the remembrance of You" (Isaiah 26:8).

RSVP Required

I enjoy making my own invitations and sending something I've made with love to specially selected friends and family. Have you ever received a personal invitation in the mail to a special tea party? Some invitations are beautiful works of art. Some promise a fun theme and an afternoon of scrumptious food and delicious teas, as well as great time with old and new friends. Usually there is a RSVP requested. "Répondez s'il vous plaît" means "respond please." A hostess wants to know if you will attend so she can adequately plan and prepare enough food for her guests. Common courtesy dictates your response.

Sadly, today many people ignore the RSVP request and fail to respond. They just set aside the invitation. We have all encountered this phenomenon when we have sent out invitations to special events such as weddings or private parties. It has led to much frustration and wonder at the lack of manners in our society today. When an invitation is ignored, an opportunity is also missed. The blessing of being personally chosen by the hostess is missed and you enjoy none of the benefits she has prepared for you.

God also invites us throughout Scripture to come to His party – to know Him and have an intimate relationship with His Son, Jesus. In the book of Isaiah God invites us all to enjoy forgiveness of sins; to come to Him and know Him without cost; to find life for our souls (Isaiah 1:18; 55:1, 3). Jesus gives the most personal invitation of all in Matthew 11:28-30. He extends it to everyone and leaves no one out. "Come to Me, all you who are weary and burdened, and I will give you rest. Take My yoke upon you and learn from Me, for I am gentle and humble in heart, and you will find rest for your souls. For My yoke is easy and My burden is light."

Jesus told the parable of a king who arranged a wedding feast for his son and invited many to attend. When his servants called on his guests, most were not willing to come and made various weak excuses. In his anger, the king said those who were invited didn't deserve to come. So he filled his tables with people he found on the streets. All who were willing to come gathered at his table and enjoyed the benefits of the feast. Jesus summed up this story with the statement: "For many are called, but few are chosen" (Matthew 22:1-14).

The chosen ones are those who respond to the invitation, "respond" being the key word. We are all invited to relationship with God, but are we willing to accept? That is our choice.

If you respond to God's invitation, He will not refuse you and you will enjoy all the benefits of personal relationship with the God of the universe (John 6:37). Jesus offers forgiveness of sins, rest for our souls and eternal life with Him. Do you really want to miss out on what God has planned for you? The pleasures and the promises of a relationship with Jesus will not be yours unless you respond to His invitation and accept it. Will you RSVP and say "yes" to Him today?

Chosen by God

Teas differ in flavor depending on several factors: soil, climate, elevation, variety and time of harvest. Some teas are packaged in a pure form; others are blended with fruits, flowers, oils, and other products to create unique blends. There are teas to please every palate. Tea plantations are cropping up in new areas of the world like Scotland, Canada, and even the San Francisco Bay Area. New companies are opening which offer fresh new blends of tea in creative packaging to attract the eye of the customer. A multitude of choices abounds!

So, imagine you are a tin of tea on a shelf in a store, one among thousands of other teas. You've been grown on a lush green bush on a mountainside in the warm sun; you've been picked, dried and processed, possibly rolled or pressed or blended; you've been shipped halfway around the globe, packaged in an attractive tin with a colorful label, and stacked on this shelf. But you have not fulfilled your purpose until someone chooses you, takes you home and uses you to steep a cup of tea.

Just as a customer chooses a tea to enjoy, so God chooses each one of us to be part of His family in Christ, His Church, and His home in heaven. The Bible tells us that God has chosen us before the foundation of the world (Ephesians 1:4). That is mind boggling to think that before God ever created time and the universe, before there was a world as we know it, He knew us and chose us individually!

What did God choose you for? He chose you for salvation through His Son Jesus Christ (2 Thessalonians 2:13-14). Peter tells us in 1 Peter 2:9-10 that God has chosen us to be holy people, His own special people, to proclaim His praises, to receive His mercy and to be the people of God who live in His marvelous light. What an amazing privilege to be called one of His chosen ones.

Looking through Scripture, we see God's choice of certain individuals. He chose Abram to leave his home in Mesopotamia and follow Him to the Promised Land—to be the father of many nations (Genesis 12:1-3; 17:1-8). God chose David, a young shepherd boy, to be a great king of the nation of Israel (1 Samuel 16:12-13). Jesus handpicked His twelve disciples to learn from Him and help carry out His mission on earth, and after His departure, to continue to preach the good news of salvation. Later, Jesus chose Paul on the road to Damascus to be His voice to the Gentiles (Acts 9:1-19; 22:12-15).

Today, God still chooses people. He chose *YOU* to be part of the family of God, to proclaim His praises to those who cross your path and to give Him glory. Jesus said, "You did not choose Me, but I chose you and appointed you that you should go and bear fruit, and that your fruit should remain, that whatever you ask the Father in My name He may give you" (John 15:16).

As you choose your next tin of tea from the shelf, remember that God has chosen you. As that tea may be a unique blend, so He has created you a unique person with a purpose to fulfill on earth. The tea's purpose is fulfilled with the steeping, bringing pleasure to the drinker. Your purpose is fulfilled when you belong to God, give Him praise and glory, and bring Him pleasure by doing His will in your life. Always remember the fact that in His infinite wisdom and mercy, He has specifically chosen YOU! Let your prayer be today that you might bring Him pleasure and fulfill His purpose for your life.

His Treasured Possession

Are you a collector of teapots and teacups? Gift shops and antique stores are filled with these beautiful items that catch our eyes and tempt us to take them home to add to our collections. Some are more difficult to pass up than others. My friend and I both have a great weakness for blue and white china as evidenced on our shelves. My particular favorites are the cobalt blue and white patterns decorated with hand painted gold accents made by Imperial Porcelain in St. Petersburg, Russia. They are my treasures.

We purchase these beauties for our collections, take them home and look forward to using them. However valuable they may be to us, they are merely objects that may in time be broken, forgotten, stolen or lost. A teacup may become a gift to a friend. Or, heaven forbid, shelves of precious china may be destroyed in an earthquake if you live on the West Coast. We keep accumulating earthly possessions, though they will someday be left behind when we step into eternity.

God Himself is a collector of sorts. His purchases are eternal and are of unfathomable value to Him. God chose the nation of Israel to be "His treasured possession" (Deuteronomy 7:6; 14:2 NIV). He continues to watch over the Jewish people. He sent Jesus Christ to them to redeem them from their sins, then made the promise of eternal life available to the Gentiles, to all who will believe.

We purchase our treasures with cash or credit cards. God has purchased us with the precious blood of His Son, Jesus Christ. We have been bought at a great price (1 Corinthians 6:20; Acts 20:28). We are God's "purchased possession" (Ephesians 1:14). "I have redeemed you; I have called you by your name; You are mine" (Isaiah 43:1). God sees us as beautiful and desires that we belong to His family. He draws us to Himself, and when we believe, He buys us as His own with the precious blood of His Son.

We look around and see temporal earthly treasures purchased with money, items that can be forgotten, ignored, stolen or destroyed. God looks around and sees precious souls that have been purchased with the blood of His Son Jesus, none of which will ever be forgotten, ignored, stolen or destroyed. He will never lose us or allow us to be taken out of His hand (John 10:28-29). God will never forget us or misplace us on a dusty shelf somewhere. We are His treasured possessions forever, and our value will never diminish in His eyes.

> How deep the Father's love for us,
> How vast beyond all measure,
> That He should give His only Son
> To make a wretch His treasure.
>
> It was my sin that held Him there
> Until it was accomplished.
> His dying breath has brought me life.
> I know that it is finished.
>
> Why should I gain from His reward?
> I cannot give an answer.
> But this I know with all my heart:
> His wounds have paid my ransom.
>
> "How Deep the Father's Love for Us," Sarah Sadler, Ignites Media

Steeped in the Word

It's tough to be a teabag. You find yourself submerged into boiling hot water and left there until all the flavor of the tea inside you is drawn out. Then you are discarded, tossed aside and thrown out with the trash. You have given your best—all that you have to give—by being steeped in hot water, but you have given yourself for another's pleasure. Your short life as a teabag has not been in vain.

Eleanor Roosevelt is often quoted as saying, "A woman is like a teabag. You can't tell how strong she is until you put her in hot water." It is true that when submerged into the "hot water" of life's difficult circumstances, challenges and trials, our true character is soon revealed. The condition of our faith is made clear. The "flavor" of our responses to trials affects those around us – either positively or negatively. Life will surely subject us to "hot water" sooner or later. How do we want to respond?

One choice is to be steeped in God's Word. Turning to His Word daily will help prepare us for the challenges life brings our way. There is wisdom and strength to be gleaned from the Scriptures. Immerse yourself in it, in all of it, both the Old and New Testaments; be filled with the knowledge of the Holy One, so that when you find yourself in life's "hot water," the flavor that emerges from your trials is one that reflects the character of Christ to others.

Paul encourages us in Romans 5:3-5 that "we glory in tribulations, knowing that tribulation produces perseverance; perseverance, character; and character, hope. Now hope does not disappoint, because the love of God has been poured out in our hearts by the Holy Spirit who was given to us." So steep yourself in God's Word, let His Holy Spirit fill you and build your character through life's trials, and have hope. Hope in God will not disappoint.

The best result of a trial by "hot water" is that God's love in you is poured out and touches those around you for His glory. Let your life be the "flavor" of God, revealed to those who are watching, all because you were first steeped in His Word. Your suffering will not have been in vain if God uses it to bless another person in need. And you will have given the best part of yourself.

Lord, help me set aside time every day to meet You in Your Word. Open my mind and my heart to what You want me to learn so I can live a life that is pleasing to You. Use the trials in my life to grow me more into the likeness of Jesus Christ. Then use me to be a blessing to someone else today. Amen.

Instructions for Life

It's almost impossible to pick up a volume dedicated to the subject of tea without finding instructions on properly preparing loose leaf tea. Different types of teas require slightly varied methods of preparation. We tend to look to all the authors of these books as "tea experts" who are in the know. We follow their directions "to a T" so to speak and then sit down to enjoy the results.

Finding dependable instructions for living life is not quite so easy. There are thousands of self-help books available from people who claim to be experts on their subjects. They can lead you down a multitude of paths that may prove helpful or not. Each author has his/her own perspective or belief system from which they offer their sage advice. So where does one begin to look for good counsel for living life? How can you choose the most reliable authority and trust their words?

If we want instructions on how to properly prepare a pot of tea, we look to one of the "tea experts" for advice. If we want instructions on how to live life, we go to God's guidebook, the Bible. This is His book of instructions for living a rich, godly life according to His standards. We accept Him as the ultimate expert and authority on righteous living.

The prophet Isaiah tells us that the Lord Almighty is "wonderful in counsel and excellent in guidance" (Isaiah 28:29). Paul states that "everything that was written in the past was written to teach us, so that through endurance and the encouragement of the Scriptures we might have hope" (Romans 15:4 NIV). David, a man after God's own heart, records God's words of assurance to him that "I will instruct you and teach in the way you should go: I will counsel you and watch over you" (Psalm 32:8 NIV).

How often do we go to Scripture to find answers or counsel from God for the challenges in our lives? Whose counsel do we follow—a human being who claims to know the best way to go or the right thing to do, or God who is "wonderful in counsel and excellent in guidance"; He who created us and knows us better than anyone else ever could?

It's not that one can't find helpful information elsewhere, but for true believers, our first choice is the Author of our faith (Hebrews 12:2a) and the Bible for our counsel. "Hold on to instruction, do not let it go; guard it well, for it is your life" (Proverbs 4:13 NIV). Though it may not always be easy, God's ways are best. In listening there is blessing.

"Whoever gives heed to instruction prospers, and blessed is he who trusts in the Lord" (Proverbs 16:20 NIV).

Lord, please continue to draw me to Your Word as I look for answers on how to live my life in a world that does not always acknowledge You or worship You. Give me discernment when others offer their advice and make Your instructions preeminent in my life. Amen.

Bread of Life

What is a tea party without a warm scone to start the party? These small, quick breads made of flour and baking powder are a traditional component of any cream or afternoon tea. They can be dropped onto griddles or baked in the oven into a variety of shapes. They can be sweet or savory and are usually made from a treasured family recipe. Scones originated in the United Kingdom, but are enjoyed all over the world today. They are traditionally served with jam, clotted cream and/or lemon curd.

Who hasn't heard the old adage, "Bread is the staff of life." It certainly was a staple in Biblical times. When Moses led the nation of Israel out of Egypt toward the Promised Land, one of the first things the people complained about was the lack of meat and bread out in the wilderness. They were used to eating bread and vegetables even though they were not their own masters in Egypt, but subject to slavery. Now in the wilderness they had none. So God in His infinite patience responded to these grumpy Israelites by giving them manna. He told them, "I will rain down bread from heaven for you" (Exodus 16:4). God provided a nutritious bread that tasted like wafers made with honey which miraculously appeared every morning. Now the people ate bread to their fill every day. God's provision sustained approximately 2 million people daily for 40 years and lasted until they stood on the threshold of the land of Canaan. They had arrived at the land of milk and honey—and plenty of bread.

God is so good to us, so faithful to provide for our needs. The Israelites needed food to sustain their bodies for 40 years of wandering and God provided the bread of heaven for them in the form of manna. Today, we each need food from heaven that will sustain us spiritually in our years of wandering on this earth. Again, our Father has provided a source of life for us through Jesus Christ, the bread of life.

John, the disciple that Jesus loved, tells us the story in chapter 6 of his gospel. Jesus had just miraculously fed over 5,000 people from just

5 loaves of bread and 2 small fish (John 6:4-14). The very next day, these same people were asking for a sign from Him so they could believe that He's been sent from God. They remembered that God gave their ancestors manna from heaven in the desert to eat. What would Jesus give them (John 6:30-31)?

Now came a teaching moment for Jesus to instruct these people about the true bread from heaven—Himself! Four times in this passage He says, "I am the bread of life—I am the bread which came down from heaven—I am the living bread." He is the true bread that God has sent to give life to the world; He gave His flesh on the cross to give us eternal life. Jesus summed up His teaching with this explanation: "This is the bread which came down from heaven—not as your fathers ate the manna and are dead. He who eats this bread will live forever" (John 6:58).

Manna sustained the Israelites physically for the duration of their 40-year march through the wilderness. A scone or two may alleviate some hunger at an afternoon tea, but Jesus sustains our spirits from now into eternity as the living bread of life. Some chose not to accept Jesus's words about who He was and left Him. Jesus turned to His 12 disciples and asked them if they would leave too. Peter's answer is one of the most poignant and powerful statements in Scripture. "Lord, to whom shall we go? You have the words of eternal life" (John 6:67-69).

Who Are You, Really?

A couple of years ago, I hosted a surprise birthday tea party for a friend. There were eight places at the table and each one had a place card with a name on it. Only the birthday guest had her own name on the card. The other seven had the first names of famous women born on the same day. On each chair was an item that gave a clue to each woman's identity. We had a great time trying to guess who each person was supposed to be from the clues. And, of course, our honored guest was made to feel as important as the "famous ladies" present at her party.

A person's identity is extremely important. We are all created unique in God's eyes. We have different personalities, different looks, different names, different life experiences and different parents, whom we may share with other siblings, yet we are still unique individuals. All these factors help shape who we are and how we think of ourselves. Just as every snowflake is unique from all the rest, so are we specially formed by the hand of the Creator, each a one-of-a-kind design.

Our identity is what makes us special, different from everyone else around us, and affirms our value as human beings. It is what makes me "me" and you "you." Poor relationships with others and traumatic experiences can warp our sense of self and leave us confused as to who we are. Many of us spend years of our lives trying to figure out who we are, and aren't even sure how to answer the question, "Who are you?" We end up describing our appearance or our experiences rather than our character and what makes our souls tick.

As Christians, Scripture tells us that if we are believers in Jesus Christ, we're saved by His death on the cross for our sins and united with Him in His resurrected life (Romans 6:5). We are new creations and our identity has been fundamentally changed (2 Corinthians 5:17, 21). So if you met a new person today who asked you to tell her about yourself, what would you say? How would you describe yourself or define who you are to this inquisitive new friend?

As one who has struggled with this question for years, I am finally comfortable with who God says I am in Christ. I am taking Him at His word!

Who am I? I am…
- A sinner saved by grace (Ephesians 2:8)
- A saint called by God (1 Corinthians 1:2)
- A citizen of Heaven (Philippians 3:20)
- A new creation (2 Corinthians 5:17)
- A child of God (John 1:12)
- Adopted into God's family (Romans 8:15; Ephesians 1:5)
- A member of Christ's Body, the Church (1 Corinthians 12:27)

How do I know this? Because God says so! The Scripture confirms it and the cross seals it. With great pleasure and confidence, I can now say, "I am a daughter of the King!"

A Vessel for His Glory

Remember the story of Alice in Wonderland? When she falls down the rabbit hole, she finds herself in a long passageway full of doors. She then embarks on a very extraordinary journey, finding along the way various items that alter her size: bottles labeled *"Drink Me"* and little cakes that have *"Eat Me"* spelled out in currants.

If your tea things could talk, what would they say? Teapots filled with steaming tea might say *"Drink Me."* Platters of tea sandwiches and bite-sized sweets might invite you to *"Eat Me."* For those of us who cherish our collections of teapots and teacups, one might hear the oft-repeated words **"Use Me."** After all, of how much use is a pretty teacup that is never filled with tea? Was it not created to be held, enjoyed and filled to bless its user rather than just collecting dust on a shelf?

So it is with us. We are all uniquely created by God for His glory. Not one of us is exactly the same. As a potter shapes a lump of clay on his wheel into a vessel of his design, so God fashions us to His own specifications and purposes.

> But now, O LORD, You are our Father;
> We are the clay, and You our potter;
> And we are all the work of Your hand (Isaiah 64:8).

> Everyone who is called by My Name,
> whom I have created for My glory;
> I have formed him, yes, I have made him (Isaiah 43:7).

As any potter soon learns, not every vessel made is perfect. Some have cracks, bubbles or other imperfections. We are all imperfect earthen vessels in bodies of flesh, some formed for noble purposes and some not. When we surrender to the Potter, He places in us the spirit of His Son, Jesus. Only He can cleanse us from the inside out and make us "useful for the Master, prepared for every good work"
(2 Corinthians 4:7; 2 Timothy 2:20-21).

Do you love the Master? Do you want to be used by Him? Are you filling yourself with the knowledge of Him through His Word? If so, then let Him use you today. Like that teacup that shouts *"Use Me,"* ask Him what He has for you to do for Him today. Is there someone who needs a phone call and a kind word? Can you offer a homebound neighbor a ride somewhere? Will you write a note of encouragement to a friend going through a difficult challenge? Or will you share the good news of Jesus and His love with someone who needs to hear it?

Let the cry of our hearts today be *"Use Me, Lord."* Then we will be fulfilling the purpose for which we were created—to bring glory to the Potter.

Tea and Friendship

Friendship and tea are good partners. A cup of tea alone with a good book is always welcome, but taking tea with a friend is special. Sitting across the table from someone you care about, sipping tea from a pretty china cup, nibbling on fresh scones with lemon curd, tea sandwiches and bite-sized sweet treats just feels so comforting. Tea is soothing and conducive to opening one's heart to another person. It can be a time of encouragement, healing or just catching up with each other—always made better accompanied by much laughter.

I just enjoyed lunch with a friend I got to know well through my tea party business. She has invited me into her home many times to share tea and scones with her friends and family. She is a blessing to me, has enriched my life through my business, and has become not only a friend, but "family" in the Lord. We did not have tea, but we "talked tea." And I am the better for it. My life is blessed, my hunger for both food and friendship is satisfied, my heart content. Time with her added joy to my day. It is so very good to have friends.

Lord, thank you for friends. Please help me be a better friend to the people you bring into my life every day. And never let me forget that You count me as a friend for whom You laid down Your life. I am blessed (John 15: 14, 15). Amen.

Here is an idea for you and a far-away friend: a **Telephone Tea Party**. Purchase some inexpensive teacups. Box up one teacup and saucer, a teabag or two, and some individually wrapped cookies (Pepperidge Farms Milanos or Walker's shortbreads are perfect). You might even tuck a silk flower for a pretty table setting and a current photo of yourself into the box. Now send it off in the mail with a note inviting your friend to tea. Arrange a time to call, make yourself a cup of tea and visit together over tea and cookies. If you prefer face time, then take tea together on Skype or your cell phones. You have provided the tea party; they have all they need to join in and you are only a phone call away.

Sharing Through Hospitality

I started collecting teapots and teacups years ago and have filled all my shelves with pieces that bring me pleasure. The more I've collected, the more I have come under conviction that it is pointless to have all these beautiful things if they are never used. They should be shared with others who will be blessed and take pleasure from them at my tea table.

Proverbs 3:9 sums it up beautifully: "Honor the Lord with your possessions." That is best accomplished when we invite people into our homes and extend hospitality to them. So one of my goals has been to open my home for afternoon tea parties and share my "tea lovelies" with friends and family. When I share the things He has given me with others, God is honored.

Paul encourages us as children of God to "practice hospitality" (Romans 12:13 NIV). What does that look like? It can be a full afternoon tea or as simple as a cup of tea and a cookie as we converse together. The important thing is that a guest feels welcome. I want people who step into my home to be blessed; to feel the presence of the Lord here and to go away feeling loved.

I particularly enjoy pampering guests at my tea table and making it an extraordinary treat for them. Most every party has a theme, a color scheme carefully laid out, a printed menu and a favor to take home. There are usually fresh flowers on the table and classical music playing softly in the background.

I once hosted three doctoral students visiting our local university from Shanghai, China. These ladies had never experienced a traditional British afternoon tea, and they were so excited. They came in, not knowing what to expect, and left with wonderful memories, a miniature white porcelain teapot, a menu and a bunch of photographs from their afternoon together. The blessing was even greater for me because of the joy I saw on their faces throughout the afternoon. These ladies were my blessing, and I am confident God was honored that afternoon.

Hospitality does not have to be that elaborate though. It is more about the people than the food or the setting. My tea table has also been a place where people have been brought together who have a common cultural heritage to meet new friends over tea and scones. Sometimes it has been an opportunity to encourage a friend who is going through a difficult situation and provide a time of stepping away from their pain for a short while to be pampered and refreshed. Once, it was to bring a few single ladies together on Valentine's Day. Hospitality can be a drink of water and a kind word, but always focused on the guest.

We all need to be loved and encouraged as we walk through life, which can be a difficult journey, filled with both joys and painful challenges. Whatever the reason someone crosses the threshold of your home, showing hospitality is of the utmost importance as a believer, to honor God and bless your guest. Having pretty tea things to create an inviting and warm reception for them is a gift from God that makes it all the more important to use the things you have and share them with others. Only then are they worth possessing.

"But do not forget to do good and to share, for with such sacrifices God is well pleased" (Hebrews 13:16).

> *"To invite a person into your house is to take charge of her happiness for as long as she is under your roof."* Anonymous

Lord, I enjoy sharing my pretty tea things with friends and family. Show me who to invite to my next tea party and help me welcome them into my home with warmth, love, and a spirit of hospitality. Amen.

Cultivating Your Spiritual Garden

Gardens by their very nature are places of cultivation. More specifically, cultivation requires knowledge, time, great attention and care to enable the plants to flourish. To experience the best results in your garden, you must prepare the soil properly; plant; fertilize; water; uproot weeds; protect your plants from pests, plant diseases and inclement weather; prune and trim; ensure proper drainage; harvest at the right time; and more. Ask any master gardener.

If you are starting a tea garden or plantation, there is much to do to cultivate the young tea plants and carefully tend them before there is a harvest of leaves to make tea. And it takes a lot of time. Tea plants can be started from seeds, cuttings or cloning leaves from "mother plants." Young tea plants spend 6-20 months in a nursery before they can be planted, depending on the climate. They are planted 3-4 feet apart and are not plucked for about 2 years, until they are 5-6 feet tall. Then they are pruned to about 3 feet tall and encouraged to spread sideways to meet the next plant, thus forming a continuous surface or "pruning plane" from which to harvest the tender leaves—all this time and effort before the plucking can even begin.

When we put our faith in Jesus Christ, He becomes our Master Gardener. There is a process of cultivation that must go on in our spiritual lives as well. Just as the tea plants must be nurtured, fed and carefully tended to mature, so must our faith in the Lord, or our spiritual garden, be nurtured, fed and carefully tended so we grow, mature and become fruitful. Initially, the Master Gardener prepares the soil of our hearts to receive the seeds of faith (Mark 4:1-20). Faith is planted in us through His Spirit, then watered and grown by the power of the Spirit through God's Word (1 Corinthians 3:6-9). Our newborn faith, like the shoots of an immature tea plant, are carefully tended: fed, protected, watered and weeded by the Master's hand as we slowly grow toward a more mature faith. The Word of God waters our souls and strengthens us; trials and the challenges of life shape us and mold us into His likeness; parts of our character that do not bear fruit are pruned like dead branches so that we might bear more fruit; and over time, we become more like the Master Gardener who lovingly cares for us (John 15:1-8).

We also have a part to play in the care and feeding of our faith. In Psalm 37, the psalmist tells us to "Trust in the Lord and do good. Dwell in the land and cultivate faithfulness." He goes on to say, "Delight yourself in the Lord and He will give you the desires of your heart. Commit your way to the Lord, trust also in Him and He will do it…Rest in the Lord and wait patiently for Him" (Psalm 37:3-7 NASB). Other Bible translations replace "cultivate" with "feed on His faithfulness" (NKJ) and "enjoy safe pasture" (NIV).

So what does it look like to cultivate faithfulness? What is our part in cultivating our spiritual garden? We are to trust, dwell, delight, commit, rest and wait on Him. We are to continue to feed and fertilize our faith by reading and studying the Word of God; dwelling in Him and fellowshipping with other believers; committing our way to Him every day; trusting in the goodness of God and His promises; resting in Him and waiting to see His hand and will in our lives. If we can do these things and place ourselves fully in the care of our Master Gardener, then we can hope to see the fruit of our spiritual gardens. Without Him, we can do nothing; but with Him, we can be as fruitful as a mature tea plant, yielding fruit in every season of our lives to the glory of God (John 15:5).

Lord, be the Master Gardener of my life. Make me the woman you want me to be so that my life bears fruit of faith that pleases You. Amen.

His Footsteps, My Pathway

Gazing over the fields of a tea plantation, row upon row of tea bushes stand, almost like soldiers marching in their ranks over the hills. Between their rows are well worn paths trod daily by the feet of workers who pluck the tea leaves. They walk the same paths during each harvest season, so the way is clearly marked for others who might come this way. If you walked these mountain paths, you would be placing your feet in the footprints of those who walked before you. What a beautiful picture of how we are to walk in the path of Jesus.

Jesus taught in His sermon on the mount that there are two paths we can take in life: the narrow way which leads to life (and few find it), or the broad way that leads to destruction (Matthew 7:13-14). The narrow path is the path of righteousness for those who follow Christ. The psalmist described it beautifully in Psalm 85:13: "Righteousness will go before Him, and shall make His footsteps our pathway."

How do we know if we're on the right path? Proverbs gives us some good advice.

> In all your ways acknowledge Him, and He shall direct your paths (Proverbs 3:6).

> The Lord guards the paths of justice, and preserves the way of His saints. Then you will understand righteousness and justice, equity and every good path (Proverbs 2:8-9).

> Let your eyes look straight ahead, and your eyelids look right before you. Ponder the path of your feet, and let all your ways be established. Do not turn to the right or the left; remove your foot from evil (Proverbs 4:25-27).

Next time you are on a path walking in the same steps of another who has gone before you, thank God that He has shown you His footsteps by the example of Jesus. Pray that they will be the pathway that you follow all the days of your life.

Robert Frost put it elegantly in his poem "The Road Not Taken."

> I shall be telling this with a sigh
> Somewhere ages and ages hence:
> Two roads diverged in a wood, and I –
> I took the one less traveled by,
> And that has made all the difference.

Which path will you choose to follow today?

Lord, show me Your footsteps in the Word so I can walk in a way that is pleasing to You. Show me the footprints of Jesus and give me grace to walk in His way. I choose the narrow way. Amen.

Photo courtesy of Harney & Sons Fine Teas

He Who Has Ears to Hear

Listening. Oh, how difficult that can be for some of us sometimes. We are so easily distracted. Well, at least I am. I think of God sitting on the throne of heaven longing to communicate with His children. He practically shouts of His presence to us through all that He has created, yet we can be so hard of hearing. We wonder at rainbows painted in the sky after a storm, yet forget the promise attached to them. We are so busy talking sometimes that we find it almost painful to silence our mouths long enough to listen to the heart of another person or to our Lord!

I have encountered groups of women at a number of tea tastings who had absolutely no intention of listening to a word I said. As I attempted to present my products and instruct them on the types of teas and how to properly prepare them, the noise level from their conversation was deafening. Trying to get their attention was a futile effort that even raising my voice or ringing a bell couldn't accomplish. I would find myself stopping mid-sentence without anyone even noticing. They just wanted to visit with each other and had no awareness that I was even speaking to them no matter how loud I spoke. What was more upsetting to me was that they were Christian, church-going women from whom I had expected some common courtesy at the very least. I felt frustrated and a little angry.

How does God feel when we refuse to listen to Him? When we're so busy or so distracted that we simply cannot hear Him? When we are just plain not interested in what He has to say about something? I'm sure it happens to us all at some point. Life can get in the way of us taking the time to just stop and listen to Him or to read His Word. At other times, we know what He would say, but we don't want to listen, so we choose rather to go our own way.

Throughout the Scriptures, God pleads with us to listen to Him. God raised up judges to deliver the Israelites time and time again from their enemies, yet the people didn't listen and continually turned back into sinful ways and had to be rescued again (Judges 2:16-17). When He spoke through the prophets, He said, "Listen carefully to Me" (Isaiah 55:2, 3). Zechariah records their response: "But they refused to pay attention; stubbornly they turned their backs and covered their ears. They made their hearts as hard as flint and would not listen to the law or to the words that the Lord Almighty had sent by His Spirit through the earlier prophets. So the Lord Almighty was very angry" (Zechariah 7:11-12 NIV). Do you blame Him? When Jesus spoke to the people about the kingdom of heaven, He often taught through the use of parables. He would challenge people by saying, "He who has ears to hear, let him hear" (Matthew 13:9; Mark 4:9, 23; Luke 8:8; 14:35). Do you hear the recurring theme?

Not listening to the wisdom and warnings from the Word can have distressing consequences for us. The Israelites wouldn't listen and experienced captivity in Babylon. When we don't listen, we experience trials that may have been avoidable and get ourselves into trouble through our sin. The Bible provides us with great wisdom from God that we would be wise to heed. In the Book of Proverbs, wisdom calls out to us saying, "Whoever listens to me will dwell safely, and will be secure, without fear of evil" (Proverbs 1:33). Again, we're urged to pay attention and listen to the sayings of the wise (Proverbs 22:17 NIV). To do that, we must be still. We can't hear Him if we're doing all the talking!

I pray that I may become more sensitive to the voice of my Savior and quiet in my spirit so I can hear Him speaking to me. With the psalmist, I purpose to "hear what the Lord will speak, for He will speak peace to His people, and to His saints" (Psalm 85:8).

Lord Jesus, please give me ears to hear today. Teach me to develop the habit of listening for Your voice. Amen.

Ah, That Fragrant Aroma!

I'm sitting at my breakfast table with my hands cupped around a mug of hot black tea. Steam from the amber liquid is rising, and I inhale it deeply. There is a pleasant, distinctive fragrance that permeates my senses, an aroma that beckons me to take that first sip. It warms me and brings me great pleasure.

Webster defines aroma as "a distinctive, pleasant fragrance." The wonderful aroma from my cup of hot tea reminds me that Jesus Christ in me is the fragrance of the knowledge of God (2 Corinthians 2:14-15). Jesus uses His children to spread this fragrance everywhere in the world around us. We are to be the fragrance of Christ among the people who cross our paths every day.

This fragrant aroma runs so much deeper than a shower and a spray of our favorite perfume. It seeps from our inner spirits and is a manifestation of Christ within us. It comes from His Spirit dwelling in us and is an offering to God as we share the knowledge of His Son with others. When Paul was imprisoned in Rome, the Philippian church sent gifts to him to minister to his needs. He commends them in his letter to the Philippians for their sacrifice which he calls "a sweet-smelling aroma, an acceptable sacrifice, well pleasing to God" (Philippians 4:18).

Jesus gave Himself sacrificially on the cross as a sweet-smelling aroma to God (Ephesians 5:2). Likewise, when we do something in the name of Jesus, either spread the good news about Him or minister to someone in His name, we give off that same sweet-smelling aroma that is so pleasing to our Father. Today let's pray that there is something we might do for Him or some word that we might speak that will touch another person with the "aroma of life leading to life" in Christ (2 Corinthians 2:16) and that our Father would inhale deeply and say, "Ah, that fragrant aroma. I am well pleased."

The Gift Giver

Don't you enjoy giving gifts to the people you love? Birthdays, anniversaries, graduations, Christmas—so many occasions to give gifts. For the tea lover, there are a multitude of enticing tea-themed gifts available. Teapots, teacups and saucers, loose leaf teas, accoutrements, tea cookies, curds and jams, and the list goes on. I have wrapped many gift sets and baskets filled with teas, scones and other treats—my favorite being a large gift basket intended for a woman suffering with cancer. It is especially exciting to receive an unexpected gift from a friend. I was just blessed with a demitasse cup and saucer of Imperial Porcelain from St. Petersburg, lovingly carried halfway around the world by a friend, just for me. How very special that made me feel!

On a Christmas years ago, my circle of friends each received a gift box from me wrapped in Christmas paper and ribbons. Inside the box were about 40 slips of paper each containing a Bible verse describing a different gift from God. It was my "God Gift Box," reminding us of so many of the gifts God loves to give to His children. I continue to discover gifts from God as I study His Word.

In fact, Scripture describes His gifts as being lavished upon us. Webster defines "lavish" as "generous and extravagant in giving." God is certainly that! He lavishes His grace and His love upon those He calls His children (Ephesians 1:8 NIV; 1 John 3:1 NIV; I John 4:9-10 NIV). He gives gifts to mankind, so many more than were in my gift box. The list gets longer every time I look into Scripture, and they are all good. James tells us in James 1:17 that "every good gift and every perfect gift is from above, and comes down from the Father of lights, with whom there is no variation or shadow of turning." He is a giver; He is constant; He gives good gifts to His children. There is nothing in our lives that is not given to us without His approval first, because He loves us so deeply.

There may be times we do not like a gift we're given, but it, too, is for a purpose in our lives. All things are filtered through God's unconditional love for us. If given a choice, our human nature would prefer life to be easy, comfortable, and convenient. However, it is not always so, and harsher for some than for others. But God remains the good gift giver in the midst of the difficulties of life, and we will see the good if we look for it (Romans 8:28). The good gifts that come to us from the hand of God far outweigh the tough stuff life can throw at us.

Next time you're wrapping that pretty teacup or a box of tea and cookies for a friend, stop to examine some of the good gifts God has given you through His son Jesus in Scripture. You will be amazed at what you find you possess in Jesus Christ. "Go shopping" for God's gifts in your Bible with a cup of tea, some paper and a pen. You'll be there a while and will come out so much the richer for it.

> He giveth more grace when the burdens grow greater,
> He sendeth more strength when the labors increase;
> To added affliction He addeth His mercy,
> To multiplied trials, His multiplied peace.
> When we have exhausted our store of endurance,
> When our strength has failed ere the day is half done,
> When we reach the end of our hoarded resources,
> Our Father's full giving is only begun.
>
> Chorus: His love has no limit, His grace has no measure, His power has no boundary known unto men; For out of His infinite riches in Jesus, He giveth, and giveth, and giveth again.
>
> From the hymn "He Giveth More Grace," Annie Johnson Flint

The King of Glory

Beauty—don't we all enjoy being surrounded by beautiful things? What joy and pleasure we experience when we walk into a room and our eyes are filled with the beauty of a perfectly set tea table. Soft music plays in the background. Silver, china and teacups are set out on fine linens, all their colors and patterns in perfect balance. Everything sparkles from the light of candles, and the air is perfumed with fresh flowers gracing the table. Our eyes are filled with beauty that invites us to sit down and enjoy this tea experience with friends.

If we were to step outside, there is much beauty to behold in nature. Tall mountains are graced by trees, quiet woods, streams and the songs of birds. Beaches are pounded by waves from the sea, and the air smells of salt; birds fill the sky with their songs, and sands of different colors squish between our toes as we search for abandoned shells. Deserts bloom with flowers in the spring and provide brilliant displays of color on otherwise drab cactus. Rainbows arch across the skies after a rain. There are a multitude of colors, textures, shapes, sizes, sounds, tastes, and moods in this world that God has created.

Yet nature is just a mere reflection of the beauty of the One who created it. God is the author and creator of beauty because He is beautiful. He is clothed in honor, majesty and light and walks on the wings of the wind (Psalm 104:1-3). King David wrote of his longing to behold the beauty of the Lord (Psalm 27:4). He is a King of glory (Psalm 24:8-10). The prophet Isaiah assures us we will see the King in His beauty (Isaiah 33:17), His glory and excellence (Isaiah 35:2b). There will come a day when all eyes will see Him, whether we believe now or not. "The glory of the LORD shall be revealed, and all flesh shall see it together" (Isaiah 40:5). Won't that day be amazing?

No beauty in this universe will compare to the beauty that will be revealed when we see our Lord face to face. Until that day, let us have eyes to see the beauty He shows us every day in the world around us in what He has created, as well as the table where we take tea. Next time you sit down at a beautiful tea table, think of the One who is the King of glory and has given us the capacity to enjoy His beauty.

"A Cup of Tea"

When the world is all at odds
And the mind is all at sea
Then cease the useless tedium
And brew a cup of tea.
There is magic in its fragrance,
There is solace in its taste;
And the laden moments vanish
Somehow into space.
And the world becomes a lovely thing!
There's beauty as you'll see;
All because you briefly stopped
To brew a cup of tea.

- William
  Gladstone

Tea by the Sea

We live in a fast-paced world that places many demands on us for our time and our energies on a daily basis. Everyone periodically needs a place to retreat to and spend time resting and renewing themselves. Even Jesus took His disciples off for a time of rest away from the demands of the crowds He ministered to every day. My special place of retreat is Pacific Grove, California. Nowhere else does it stir my heart to worship the Lord as much as by the beautiful sea, especially at Pt. Lobos Marine Reserve just south of Carmel. I have spent a multitude of hours hiking the breathtaking trails on this gorgeous stretch of rocky beach and cypress forest. Some days the warm sun is brightly shining, and other days the fog is rolling down toward the shore from over the tops of the cypress trees like a blanket of white cotton candy. The water can be a deep royal blue or a pool of soft emerald green pulsing with each wave that rolls in. The air is filled with the barks of sea lions, the calls of gulls, and the scent of salt and

sea weed. Deer occasionally make an appearance among the trees or gather on a quiet stretch of trail. God is definitely in this place!

In college I took a fascinating Marine Biology course. We used a textbook entitled *This Great and Wide Sea* to study tides and currents. I was surprised one day to find the title in Scripture! "This great and wide sea, in which are innumerable teeming things, living things both small and great" (Psalm 104:25). One day "the earth will be filled with the knowledge of the glory of the Lord, as the waters cover the sea" (Habakkuk 2:14; Isaiah 11:9). At creation, God determined the size of the seas and set the limits of how far the waves could reach. "This far you may come, but no farther, and here your proud waves must stop" (Job 38:8-11; Psalm 33:7; Proverbs 8:29). The One who created the oceans and all that is in them walked on the waters of the Sea of Galilee and left invisible footprints on the surface of the water. "Your way was in the sea, Your path in the great waters, and Your footsteps were not known" (Psalm 77:19). He can stir the waters so their waves roar or still them with a word (Jeremiah 31:35; Psalm 65:7; Matthew 8:23-27). One has only to open their eyes to see God's presence by the sea.

On a cold, windy hike, I like to find a big rock overlooking the sea and take time to sit with my Bible and some hot tea. On warm days, a beach chair and a big glass of iced tea is the perfect way to spend an afternoon with the Lord and ponder who He is and the world He has made. On one visit to the local lighthouse in Pacific Grove, I spied two old tea sets used by former lighthouse keepers. Here you see one set on a table overlooking the shoreline. What a cozy spot for a morning devotion and time in the Word.

My spirit is inspired by the sea. I have lain on a sandy beach with a friend and brainstormed on all the ways the ocean reminds us of God. He is constant, cleansing, healing, powerful, cannot be contained, immeasurably vast, filled with life, reflects His glory on the water, and on it goes. I have stood beside breaking waves at night and sung praises to God with another friend. I have spent hours sitting on a rock with paper and pen, pouring out my heart to God. I have been awed by incredible sunsets that God has painted on the skies and equally enjoyed the moon reflecting like diamonds off the water as it slowly sets into the sea. To me, those times were a glimpse of the face of God.

Next time you need to get away, I heartily recommend a trip to the sea. Be sure to take your Bible, paper and pen, and a big container of tea. Be ready to meet with God, because He will definitely be waiting for you there. Today is a good day for taking tea by the sea.

Is Anybody Home?

It can be an uncomfortable feeling to arrive at someone's home where you are expected, see the lights on, and begin knocking, yet no one comes to the door to open it and let you in. You might start wondering if you have the right day, are there at the right time, or even have the right house. You think to yourself, "Where is everybody? I'm here!"

When I scheduled tea tasting parties for my business, my hostesses were always instructed to expect me one hour before the party was to begin. I needed that amount of time to set up my product display, prepare the teas for steeping, warm the teapots and boil the water. It also gave me time to reconnect with my hostess, review the order of events for the party, and answer any questions she might have.

One afternoon, I arrived at my destination at the appointed time, unloaded my bags from the car, and knocked on the door. The lights were on inside and I was expected. However, there was no answer. I continued to knock and wait. Then I knocked again and waited. I continued knocking, a little harder each time with no results but the barking of 3 dogs on the other side of the door. So where was everyone? Was anybody home? After a full 5 minutes of knocking, which felt like an eternity, my hostess's husband slowly made his way to the door, threw it open, then retreated upstairs before I was even inside. Apparently, both her husband and daughter were home, but didn't feel any urgency to answer the front door. The hostess had left to run to the grocery store just before I was due to arrive. I did not feel very welcome.

I often wonder if this is how Jesus feels when He stands at the door of someone's life, knocking to be let in, yet no one will open the door to Him. I visualize Him standing there knocking and maybe raising His voice to inquire, "Hello! Is anybody home?" He longs for people to open the doors of their lives to Him so He can have an intimate relationship with each one. He says, "Behold, I stand at the door and knock. If anyone hears My voice and opens the door, I will come in to him and dine with him, and he with Me" (Revelation 3:20). Yet He isn't always welcome.

What does His knocking sound like? Looking back on a time when I know now He was knocking on the door of my life, it had many different sounds. He had been knocking on my door from my childhood, witnessing to me of His existence through His incredible creation (Romans 1:20). He knocked through the Holy Spirit who was drawing me in the deepest parts of my soul, revealing the depth of my need for Him. He knocked through the New Testament Scriptures which I felt compelled to read. He knocked through the lives of Christian women who were praying for me and walking beside me through some painful circumstances. He even knocked on my heart through some of the liturgy of the church I was raised in from my youth, which I began to question, and through a college course that taught things that were contrary to what Scripture said about God. The difficult part was recognizing that all these things were God trying to get my attention. God approaches each of us in different ways and by means perfectly tailored to reach us as unique individuals. Everyone's story of their encounter with Him is different and personal. Jesus had to knock very loudly for a very long time before I was even aware it was Him.

We humans tend to build up walls around ourselves for protection. We do allow select people into our lives through a sort of door that we can open or close at our discretion. We are the doorkeepers and control the opening and closing of this door to our innermost being. This is the door that Jesus stands before and knocks as our Shepherd. It is up to us to open it and let Him in or leave Him standing outside. "He who enters by the door is the shepherd of the sheep. To him the doorkeeper opens, and the sheep hear his voice" (John 10:2-3). Jesus said, "If anyone loves Me, he will keep My word; and My Father will love him, and We will come to him and make Our home with him" (John 14:23). But for this to happen, the doorkeeper must open the door.

If you hear Jesus knocking on the door of your heart, why not swing that door open, welcome Him in to your life, and let Him make His home with you? For me, when I opened that door, my life changed and has never been the same since. He brought with Him not only forgiveness, but companionship, love, peace, joy, comfort, security, and a hope that will not disappoint (Romans 5:5). Today, is He knocking on your door? He won't bang on it, but gently knock, so I hope you're listening.

Words of My Mouth

Language is a tool God has created as a means of communication. He designed us to communicate with Him and with each other through the spoken and the written word. Our ability to use both spoken and written language sets us apart from animals and reflects the image of our Creator. In Scripture, we see God writing His commandments as "with the finger of God" on the stone tablets of Moses (Exodus 31:18). Later, we see Jesus writing something on the ground before the accusers of a woman caught in adultery (John 8:1-11). Fortunately for us today, God instructed His chosen ones to record His words in written form, so we may know our God in this present age through the Bible.

Words can be very powerful: they can comfort and build up; they can accuse and tear down; they can make us laugh and make us cry; they encourage us or disappoint us; they can be filled with truth or deceive with lies.

Sometimes our lips seem to take on a life of their own and our words can come out all wrong at the worst possible times. At one of my tea parties, I was presenting a holiday tea blended with orange peel, though it came out of my mouth as "orange people." Easily embarrassed, it took me a few minutes to recover. Another time I was meeting with one of my team members on an evening when we were both very tired. In discussing some teas that were going to be discontinued and only available in limited quantities, I said they would be in limited "quality." My friend replied, "That's why they are being retired, Sue." She then, with her own slip of the tongue, proceeded to mispronounce our Peppermint Twist tea as, "Peppermint Sh*t, my favorite tea!" Needless to say, we had an evening filled with hearty laughter and found it best to quit while we were ahead, stop talking, and go home to bed. (I had a fleeting thought that we could form our own comedy team and take this on the road!)

My mind is constantly filled with words. Some of them are quick to slip past my lips before I can catch them, and they can have a devastating effect on someone if they are not spoken in love. Sad to say, that is not always the case. How many times I have listened to the words that have come out of my mouth and instantly wished I could retract them! But alas, once past the lips, it's too late. If only my mind and my lips could get it together with my spirit before they share my thoughts! Many mornings I find myself praying with the psalmist, "Set a guard, O Lord, over my mouth; keep watch over the door of my lips" (Psalm 141:3). I pray that the Lord will guard what comes out of my mouth and, if necessary, restrain my lips with a spiritual muzzle (Psalm 39:1). I picture the Holy Spirit's hand over my mouth, saving me from myself.

I purpose in my heart not to sin with my mouth (Psalm 17:3), though James tells us that our tongues are mighty weapons that cannot be tamed and can be unruly (James 3:6-10). This is where self-control comes in; that I might think before I speak. I pray for more of this fruit of the Holy Spirit in me (Galatians 5:22-23). I long to use this gift of language to encourage and affirm others rather than cause them hurt. "Whoever guards his mouth and tongue keeps his soul from troubles" (Proverbs 21:23). Wise words indeed!

So my prayer now becomes, "May these words of my mouth and this meditation of my heart be pleasing in Your sight, O Lord, my Rock and my Redeemer" (Psalm 19:14 NIV). Beginning each day with words of praise for God puts me on the right path to step into my day. "And my tongue shall sing aloud of Your righteousness. O Lord, open my lips, and my mouth shall show forth Your praise" (Psalm 51:14-15).

Father, today may my words be used to communicate encouragement and affirmation to others, and be flavored with grace. Amen.

Engraved on the Palms of His Hands

Over the years I have discovered certain china patterns that I particularly like in antique stores or tea shops. I usually save a photo or make a note of the pattern with its name and cost to tuck away for future reference, hoping that I might add it to my collection down the road. You may do the same thing.

Have you ever been caught without paper when you just have to write something down you dare not forget? What do you do? Many people will jot a note on the palm of their hand so they can transfer it later to paper. Just don't forget to transfer it to something more permanent before you wash your hands.

God keeps track of things in writing too. He never forgets those who are His own because He engraves our names on the palms of His hands. In the Old Testament, He gave Israel this assurance through the prophet Isaiah: "Can a mother forget the baby at her breast and have no compassion on the child she has borne? Though she may forget, I will not forget you! See, I have engraved you on the palms of my hands. Your walls are ever before me" (Isaiah 49: 15-16). God couldn't forget them even if He tried. He would see them every time He opened His hands.

The New Testament gives us a similar image—the nail marks on the hands of Jesus Christ. These nail marks that Jesus bears are for our sin. Paul tells us in Colossians 2:13-14 when we were dead in our sins because of our sinful nature, Jesus took our sin upon Himself and died in our place on the cross. The punishment for our sin? "He took it away nailing it to the cross." If we accept this free gift, our sins are forgiven. However, it has left permanent nail scars on Christ's hands and feet.

When we picture His scarred hands, we can see ourselves and what should have been our punishment. We see our names in those precious marks because we know our sin was present there when Roman soldiers drove those nails into His flesh. Jesus will forever bear nail marks that remind us of the awesome thing He did so we could live and not be subjected to that punishment.

Thomas, one of His disciples, was not present the first time the resurrected Christ came to the disciples. After hearing their report, Thomas said, "Unless I see the nail marks in His hands and put my finger where the nails were, and put my hands into His side, I will not believe it." One week later, Jesus came to the disciples again and put all of Thomas's doubts to rest. He did not rebuke Thomas, but compassionately invited him to touch His wounded hands and side. "Stop doubting and believe." Can you even begin to imagine the power of that moment in Thomas's life? What more could the man say than, "My Lord and My God"? He was forever changed in that powerful moment (John 20:24-28).

When we see Jesus face to face, He will still bear those nail marks. He was nailed and wounded for you and me. He placed our sin on that cross. When He looks at His scars, He sees you and me. What an awesome moment that will be when we bow at His feet and say, "My Lord and My God."

Lord, please remind me every time I wash my hands that my name is ever before Your eyes. You will not forget me. Let that be a comfort to me today. Amen.

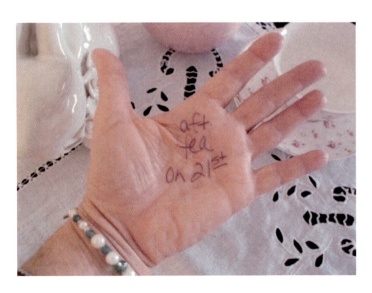

The Everlasting Arms

Have you ever stopped to think about all the things you do every day with your arms? Our arms embrace loved ones, cuddle babies close to our hearts and comfort the hurting with hugs. We use our arms to bathe, to dress, to cook, to feed ourselves, and to carry groceries and laundry. We lift our arms in worship in church. We extend our arms in greeting, raise them in school to ask questions, wrap them around ourselves to keep warm and use them to defend ourselves from potential harm. We lift weights to make our arms stronger and hope they brace us if we stumble. They are the perfect tools to lift a cup of tea to our lips.

Scripture speaks of the arms of God as well. When Moses questioned God about His provision for the Israelites in the wilderness, God asked him if he thought God's arm was too short to handle this miracle. Obviously, not (Numbers 11:23). The prophet Isaiah painted this word picture of God: "He tends His flock like a shepherd: He gathers the lambs in His arms and carries them close to His heart" (Isaiah 40:11 NIV). When Jesus walked the earth, He gathered children in His arms and blessed them (Mark 10:16). I know He does the same for us today because of His great love for us.

I had been asked to address a group of professional and very accomplished women at an afternoon tea at a museum. They wanted me to discuss thousands of years of tea history in just ten minutes – an impossible task! I spent over a month preparing and paring down my presentation, and then practicing until it became familiar enough that I didn't need to rely so heavily on my notes. I have never in my life been in any way comfortable speaking in front of people. As the event loomed in front of me, my anxiety was tangible. I wanted to do my very best and not feel foolish in front of these business women, some of whom were professors and even a judge.

The tea was scheduled for a Sunday afternoon, and that morning God did something amazing for me. He gave me a crystal clear picture that flashed into my mind in the midst of singing hymns in church. I saw Jesus standing strong and tall behind me with His arms surrounding me and His hands resting on my hands as I held my notes. What a precious gift He had given me—a picture of being enveloped in His presence and a comfort that eased my anxiety. He would be with me, and that made all the difference. I was able to address my audience with a minimum of nerves and tumbles over my tongue.

I now had a much more real and personal understanding of what the psalmist said in Psalm 139:5: "You hem me in—behind and before; You have laid Your hand upon me." His arms supported me as I gave my presentation, just as Moses declared: "The eternal God is your refuge, and underneath are the everlasting arms" (Deuteronomy 33:27).

This was a hug from God—just for me. In the big scheme of things, my anxiety about speaking to a few women about tea seemed much too small an issue for God to take time away from the problems of the world to help me. But God is the strength of my heart when my flesh and my heart fail me (Psalm 73:26). He cares for me enough to comfort me when anxiety and fear threaten to overwhelm me.

To Him I am not insignificant, and He took the time to show me that I am wrapped in His arms. A small plaque on my bedroom wall is another reminder of the arms of Jesus:

> "I asked Jesus, 'How much do You love me?' 'This much,' He answered, and He stretched out His arms and died."

Worth the Wait

Do you hate standing in long lines that don't move? Do you get impatient waiting for the seeds you've planted in your garden to sprout, mature and produce flowers? Are you anxious for those chocolate chip cookies in the oven to finish baking? If you're like me, the answer is a resounding "YES!" In the times we live in, most of us in our society are conditioned to expect immediate gratification, instant food from the microwave, and instant communication via our cell phones. We watch instant replays on TV, pick up our lunch at a drive through, and travel much too fast on our freeways. It's no wonder that we are not very good at waiting. It seems that the only place we will voluntarily step into an outrageously long, slow-moving line is in Disneyland! And even then we prefer the Fast Pass. We are a people in a hurry to get wherever we're going, but losing the ability to enjoy the journey.

It's much that way with preparing a good cup of loose leaf tea. You first wait for the water to boil. You prepare your tea leaves in an infuser to be steeped. Then when the water is poured over the leaves, again you wait the required amount of time for proper steeping. At the most, this might take ten minutes of your time, but for some this is just too inconvenient. We want to just dunk a tea bag into hot water from the microwave long enough for it to turn the water a caramel color. Or worse yet, we pour loose tea granules into water for that "instant" glass of iced tea or open a bottle of ready-to-drink tea. But what is instant is not always gratifying. What is gained by rapid results is often at the expense of flavor and the soothing calm that accompanies the process of a well prepared cup of tea.

Searching through the Scriptures, there are at least 56 verses that address this issue of waiting. We are instructed to "watch," "look for," and "wait" for God to show up in our world and in our lives. We who believe in Jesus Christ are to be people who expectantly hope and eagerly wait for God to reveal Himself to us. And God says, "They shall not be ashamed who wait for Me" (Isaiah 49:23). If we are to get up close and personal with God, then we must be willing to wait on Him. He is not an "instant" God and will not conform to our impatient time tables. He will show up in His time and cultivate patience (one of the fruits of the Spirit) in us as we learn to wait on Him (Galatians 5:22-23).

Waiting on God reminds me of a flowering tea. These tea balls are works of art created by hand in China. Tea leaves are tightly tied around a flower and compressed into a tight ball. It takes time and patience to create a tea blossom, but it is well worth the wait. Flowering teas are steeped in glass teapots so the process of the leaves slowly unfolding in hot water to reveal the beautiful flower within can be observed and enjoyed. It can become the centerpiece of your tea table. Like these lovely teas, God slowly teaches us, reveals Himself to us, and changes us over time and through trials, our version of "hot water."

As Christians, we eagerly wait for the revelation of our Lord (1 Corinthians 1:7). We rest in the Lord and wait patiently for Him (Psalm 37:7). We look for the mercy of our Lord Jesus Christ (Jude 21). We eagerly wait for the adoption, the redemption of our bodies (Romans 8:23). We wait for the blessed hope and glorious appearing of our Savior Jesus Christ (Titus 2:13; Hebrews 9:28). And we look for new heavens and a new earth in which righteousness will dwell (2 Peter 3:13).

What are you waiting and hoping for today? Waiting can be difficult, but with God, however He shows Himself is well worth the wait. Remember the words of Isaiah. "Those who wait on the Lord will renew their strength. They shall mount up with wings like eagles. They shall run and not be weary. They shall walk and not faint" (Isaiah 40:31). So with David, we know that eventually we will see the goodness of God in the land of the living if we keep our eyes open (Psalm 27:13). And it will be well worth waiting for!

Lord, help me to keep my eyes open as I wait to see Your hand at work in my life today. Don't let me miss seeing what You are doing in my life and the lives of those whom I love. Encourage me with glimpses of You and renew my hope each day. Thank you. Amen.

Broken Before God

Have you ever broken one of your favorite teapots or teacups? I have several teacups that have had the handles broken off in a careless moment. Though the handles are repaired with strong glue, I can't trust those cups to ever hold hot tea again. So they are relegated to the back shelf, to be used for some other purpose. An occasional teapot has also been broken or cracked, now to be used as a decorative vase for flowers on my tea table or a planter in my garden.

Like my teacups, we are broken and damaged human beings. Have you ever thought about what it means to be human and broken? Webster defines broken as "separated violently into parts; shattered." Sin separates us from God and causes pain and grief in our relationships. We become broken-hearted, that is "overcome by grief or despair." Our will is broken, and our heart is shattered. Our own strength and self-will alone are not sufficient to overcome the trials and temptations of life on this planet. And glue cannot fix these problems.

Why do we experience brokenness? We are strong enough, aren't we? We can do life our way, can't we? Well, let's put it this way: if God did not allow people to be overwhelmed and feel powerless, to be broken in spirit, who would ever need Him? If we did not come to the end of ourselves at some point, why would we turn to Him? If we could not be broken, we might never recognize or admit our need for God. God's kingdom would be sparsely inhabited and many church pews empty. This is part of what it means to be human: to recognize our need.

Some of us feel so broken that we may even despair of life. When we reach this point, we have a choice to make: fall on our knees and cry out to God, or consider other inadequate and ineffective methods to stop the pain. As other broken people have done before us, many of them in Scripture, they have chosen to turn to God. Only He has the answers we seek.

We know we need God. It is our brokenness that moves us to cry out to Him. Brokenness leads us to the cross of Jesus Christ, and brokenness keeps us there. The good news is that…

> The Lord is near to those who have a broken heart (Psalm 34:18a).
>
> He heals the broken hearted and binds up their wounds (Psalm 147:3).

Jesus comes to our rescue and becomes the glue that holds us together; He heals our brokenness. He does not put us on a back shelf, possibly to be forgotten or never used again. Instead He makes us whole. He has a purpose for our lives. Scripture is filled with stories of people who were broken and despaired of life, some as a result of their own sins—David, Jonah, Elijah, Peter and many others whom God loved. If these great people of God experienced brokenness, how should we expect to avoid it if we want to be close to Him? We shouldn't mind those "cracks" in our lives anymore, because they remind us of Who we belong to and that He will find a use for us in His kingdom in spite of them. So pick up that cracked teacup and find another purpose for it. It is still beautiful!

Lord, please remind me every day that I am only whole because of You. Shine Your light through the "cracks" in my life and use the things I've learned by being broken to bless others. Amen.

Lay That Burden Down

My tea cup is filled this morning with a strong, malty Assam tea that comes from the largest tea-growing region on earth. It is grown on a tropical plain in the region of Assam in Northeast India, adjacent to Bangladesh and Myanmar, and borders the Brahmaputra River. The tea's strong malty flavor is perfect for adding milk and has a very distinctive flavor. It is one of my favorites.

In Assam, tea leaves are traditionally harvested by women. They grasp the first two leaves and a bud between the thumb and the tip of the third finger, carefully break them off in a quick downward movement, and then throw them over their shoulders into a basket or bag carried on their backs from a strap that rests across their foreheads. When filled, the baskets are carried to a collection spot where they are emptied, and the women return to the fields to continue picking. Their baskets can weigh up to 45 pounds when they are full, according to a grower I met at a tea festival. He said the women will fill their baskets twice a day, working their way up and down the mountains.

I don't think most tea drinkers realize the hard physical labor invested in a cup of tea. This is tedious labor. I cannot imagine how difficult and uncomfortable it would be to stand in the hot sun all day long with a heavy basket balanced on my back with the pressure of the band resting on my forehead. What a burden these women carry every day as they labor so I can have my tea every morning. I, for one, am very appreciative. I know that I could not do this work.

Many of us carry similar "burdens" through life that may be the guilt of past sins, the worries of life, fears of the future, or the trauma of others' sins committed against us. This too is hard work. But we are not meant to carry burdens such as these if we have Jesus as our Lord and Savior. As Christian was delivered of his burdens in the story *Pilgrim's Progress* by John Bunyan, so God can deliver us of the burdens weighing us down. The Book of Psalms is filled with encouragement and hope regarding these burdens.

> Praise be to the Lord, to God our Savior, who daily bears our burdens (Psalm 68:19 NIV).
>
> Cast your burden on the Lord and He shall sustain you (Psalm 55:22).
>
> The Lord upholds all those who fall and lifts up all who are bowed down (Psalm 145:14).

Isn't it good to know we do not need to carry this weight all alone? We can give these burdens to Him who is able to carry them for us and free us from being weighed down. Let Him have the things in your life today that are just too heavy for you to bear. Allow Him to lift you up and take that weight upon Himself. He is able and loves you enough to walk alongside you through this day, taking on the burden for you.

Photo courtesy of
Dan Robertson,
The Tea House/World Tea Tours

A Cup of Chaos

When I plan a tea party, I think of a peaceful setting: a pretty tea table, fresh flowers, soft music playing in the background, all designed to create an inviting place to slow down, gather with friends and family, and connect with each other over a cup of tea and some treats. A quiet room sets the stage for intimate conversation and enjoyment for the people around the table. It's difficult to enjoy an afternoon tea when there is noise and chaos swirling around you.

I experienced this "cup of chaos" at one of my tea tastings. I was at a friend's home to display tea wares and share tea and scones with her guests. As I attempted to set up my product display and prepared the tea to steep for the party, it felt like complete chaos around me. There were two dogs and a cat running loose around the room getting underfoot, one a beagle who continuously howled through most of the party. The heat was turned up so high that I could barely breathe. As I worked at my table, my friend's dad was vacuuming the room around me, as well as the fireplace, so he could light a fire. Then he proceeded to mop the kitchen floor with PineSol just as I needed access to the kitchen to steep tea. The strong smell nearly choked me. On top of the noise of the barking dogs and the vacuum, jazz music was playing so loudly that we had to shout at each other to be heard. Eventually, I had to request that the music be turned off so I could speak to the guests without shouting.

Along with the dogs, there were several husbands, fathers and brothers in and out. They wanted to taste the teas, but left when the guests arrived. Then came the comments from one guest about how much she disliked tea and went so far as to arrange someone to call her phone as an excuse for her to leave the party early. I always wonder when people come to a tea party adamantly declaring how much they dislike tea. Why did they even come? The men did return at the end of the afternoon to finish off the remaining tea and scones.

Needless to say, the chaos of these few hours left me stressed and totally spent.

Thank goodness Jesus does not offer us a "cup of chaos." He is called our Prince of Peace for a reason (Isaiah 9:6). The psalmist promises great peace to those who love God's Word (Psalm 119:165). He says, "I will hear what God the Lord will speak, for He will speak peace to His people" (Psalm 85:8). That is so good to know when the world around us seems to be careening out of control. Persecution, wars, protests, violence, poverty, anger and hatred swirl around us and confront us head-on every time we read the newspaper or listen to the news. We need to know where we can find peace to soothe our weary souls.

The Prince of Peace, Jesus Christ, is the answer for those seeking peace in chaotic times. Paul teaches that "He Himself is our peace" (Ephesians 2:14a). Isaiah tells us that God will keep us in perfect peace when our minds are focused on Him and we place our trust in Him (Isaiah 26:3). Jesus Himself left us His promise to comfort us in the chaos and trials of life: "Peace I leave with you; My peace

I give you. I do not give to you as the world gives. Do not let your hearts be troubled and do not be afraid" (John 14:27 NIV). "I have told you these things, so that in Me you may have peace. In this world you will have trouble. But take heart! I have overcome the world" (John 16:33 NIV). What an amazing promise to comfort our hearts when we long for peace and serenity.

When you most need to experience His peace, steep a cup of tea, find a quiet place, and let Him speak to your heart. "And the peace of God, which surpasses all understanding, will guard your hearts and minds through Christ Jesus" (Philippians 4:7). A cup of tea with the King beats the "cup of chaos" the world offers every time.

Soul Spa

One Christmas season, I spent an entire Saturday serving tea and scones to customers and staff at a day spa. I came before the spa opened and set up a tea shop in the foyer next to a water fountain. The area was beautifully decorated for the Christmas season, and the sound of the water created a relaxing setting. Clients were greeted at the door with a hot cup of fragrant tea, a small cinnamon scone and a warm welcome.

Day spas are places where women go to be pampered—to have manicures, pedicures, facials, massages and whatever other services are provided there. It is all geared to beautify the outside of a woman, to improve and maintain her appearance. The Bible comments on the outward beauty of women: Abraham's wife Sarah, "a woman of beautiful countenance" (Genesis 12:11); Rebekah, the wife of Isaac, who "was beautiful to behold" (Genesis 24:16); Bathsheba, the very beautiful woman who eventually became the wife of David and mother of Solomon (2 Samuel 11:2); and the "lovely and beautiful" Esther who became queen to the King of Persia (Esther 2:7b).

In Biblical times, there were some very elaborate beauty treatments for women, the most notable being the beauty preparations young women had to go through before being presented to the King of Persia. These young beauties went through 12 months of "preparations for beautifying women." Only then were they ready to be taken before the King for his selection of his next queen (Esther 2:12).

Don't most women want to feel beautiful on the outside? We spend money on cosmetics, hair salons, exercise programs, jewelry and clothing so we look our best. But Proverbs 31:30 tells us that beauty is fleeting. No matter how hard we work at it, age will overtake us and our bodies will change. Youth will transition into old age and it will become more difficult to maintain our outer beauty. Fortunately, God looks at us differently. "For the Lord does not see as man sees; for man looks at the outward appearance, but the Lord looks at the heart"

(1 Samuel 16:7). God takes pleasure not in physical strength, but in those who fear Him and put their hope in His mercy (Psalm 147:10-11). You can have a makeover for your body at the spa, but God gives us a makeover for our soul that makes us beautiful within.

The psalmist said the Lord "will beautify the humble with salvation" (Psalm 149:4). He sets His Holy Spirit within us when we believe and begins a new beauty routine that changes our hearts. "The unfading beauty of a gentle and quiet spirit, which is of great worth in God's sight," (1Peter 3:3-4 NIV) becomes of much greater value than how we look. To God, the state of our hearts is far more significant than our looks or how well we're groomed.

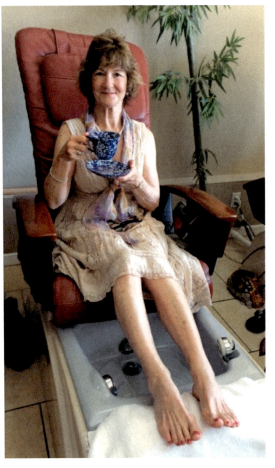

Even if we go through a year of beauty routines like Esther did, we are not "just another pretty face." Our value to God is reflected in our hearts and our character. "The King will greatly desire your beauty" (Psalm 45:11a), but it will be the inner beauty of your heart and spirit. Are you spending time with the Lord in His soul spa? Are you allowing Him to beautify your heart through His Word? We would do well to take the time to immerse ourselves in God's beauty treatment for our souls. Remember, to the King, *you are beautiful!*

Comfort in a Cup

Tea has long been associated with comfort. From childhood, the promise of comfort and warmth was a gift from my mother when I didn't feel well, always presented in a cup of tea with honey and lemon. Tea sets the mood for slowing down, taking a deep breath, and spending quiet time—with God, a good book, or a good friend. It is comfort in a cup.

One of my customers reminded me of this very thing. Exactly two years after meeting her at an event I hosted, she called me to discuss a plan she had dreamed up with her co-workers. She was the charge nurse in the neonatal unit of a local hospital. She and her fellow nurses wanted to be able to serve tea to parents who had lost a newborn infant, to offer a cup of comfort in a painful situation. Cost was no object compared to being able to offer comfort to grieving parents through the simple gesture of steeping a cup of tea and serving them in their hospital room. She purchased everything she would need for a tea service: a white teapot, two white teacups, teaspoons, a creamer and sugar bowl, all to be presented on a pretty white tray. It was deeply touching to me that these nurses had such compassion for grieving parents suffering this kind of a loss and wanted to express their compassion through this gesture. As further validation of this kindness, a study done at City University London confirmed that even a single cup of tea can significantly reduce anxiety levels after suffering a stressful experience.[3] So these nurses had the right idea.

God is a comforter too. He is "The Father of compassion and the God of all comfort, who comforts us in all our troubles" (2 Corinthians 1:3-4 NIV). He comforts the downcast (2 Corinthians 7:6 NIV). Jesus promised that "blessed are those who mourn, for they will be comforted" (Matthew 5:4 NIV). When your heart is breaking and you've experienced a loss in your life, you can go to God's Word and find comfort in His presence.

We all need to know that someone cares about our suffering of soul, and we are assured of that in the Scriptures. The psalmist declared, "May Your unfailing love be my comfort," and "I remember, Lord, Your ancient laws, and I find comfort in them" (Psalm 119: 52, 76 NIV). God assures His people that, "I, even I, am He who comforts you" (Isaiah 51:12 NIV).

If you are in need of comfort and assurance that you are loved in the midst of grief or pain and that you are not left to suffer alone, steep a cup of tea and spend time with the God of all comfort. He has arms big enough to wrap around your soul and hold you tightly until the darkness passes by.

Tea for Two

Lined up across my mantle are four tea-for-one sets. They have attractive blue and white designs and are ideal for the solitary tea drinker. One can steep their favorite tea leaves in the small pot and enjoy it from the matching cup that makes the base of the set. It's perfect tea ware for one to enjoy an afternoon tea break with a few tea cookies.

I have lived most of my adult life alone. I've had my share of roommates, but my preference is to have my own private space to call home. So a tea-for-one set should be perfect for me. However, I prefer tea for two.

I have worked all my life and was always around people during the work week. My last 16 years were spent at a private university where I was surrounded by staff, faculty, and an ever-changing body of students every day. Now I am newly retired and find myself longing to be around people more. I miss interacting with students, helping people who stop by my desk, and providing a listening ear to co-workers. As I write this, I am experiencing that old longing again—to have an intimate companion with whom to share my life.

When Jesus was preparing His disciples for His departure, He spoke tenderly to them knowing His death would cause them grief. He told them He would not leave them alone but would come to them (John 14:18). They would see Him again. He also assured them that, "If anyone loves Me, he will keep My Word; and My Father will love him, and We will come to him and make Our home with him" (John 14:23).

I need to be reminded when I feel lonely that I am not alone. Jesus, the Father, and the Holy Spirit made their home in me when I first believed. Though I only see my face in the mirror, I can rest in the fact that I am part of the household of God and He is near. When I pull out my tea-for-one and steep myself a cup of tea, it is not just for me. I open my Bible, listen to the words of God, and have a time of tea for two, just myself and my Lord.

King David wrote, "God sets the lonely in families" (Psalm 68:6 NIV). I do not have my own family, but am still privileged to have my parents, sister, niece, and extended family in my life. God has been so good to me through the last 40 years in His household to make a place for me to share in the lives of other families at various times. I have plenty of friends and acquaintances to spend time with, but it is the quiet times at home that can get lonely.

So how do I handle those lonely times? I go somewhere to be around people. I try to find something I can do for someone else. Or I just steep some tea and have tea for two with Jesus. He is my family, and He is always free for tea.

Lord, when I am feeling lonely, please help me discern if it's people I need or You. Are You calling me to spend more time with You or to go minister to someone else? Are You wanting to speak with me alone or send me out to do Your will and bless someone else? Please make my path clear and guide me in Your way. Amen.

Let the Children Come

There is just something so special about little girls: all dressed up in frilly dresses and shiny shoes, bows in their hair and giggles of excitement because they are going to a tea party! Is this their first tea party? Have they any idea what to expect? Do they even know what tea is? Does it really matter? They know that this is something very special because they are dressed in their finest clothes and they are bursting with excitement and expectation. Isn't that how Jesus wants us to feel about spending time with Him?

I have had the pleasure of serving a number of children at some of my tea parties. Some were as young as 2 years old, and one a young man of 13. He actually liked tea and took notes during my presentation. The little girls were usually in dresses and sat at small tables enjoying their herbal tea and sandwiches and using their best table manners. One group of "royal" young ladies was wearing dresses of different Disney princesses. Another special young lady has been to my home at least four times for afternoon tea since she was 2 years old, the last time being a special tea-for-two. When my niece was about 4 years old, she brought all of her teddy bears to visit and we had a Teddy Bear Tea Party in the garden. That's one memory I cherish!

I prefer to not refuse requests for children to attend tea parties if at all possible. I will set out miniature cups and saucers and serve them tea in tiny teapots. I believe we make wonderful memories for our children when we take the time to have them to tea. Several grandmothers I know make a point of creating those special moments with their granddaughters over tea time that hopefully will continue into adulthood. Establishing a family tradition of afternoon tea is a fantastic way to bond and build relationships with our children. It is pouring blessing into their lives. It is also an opportunity to talk with them about Jesus and how much He loves them. So let the little children come.

Jesus took a strong stand on welcoming children. He made time for them and never turned them away. When parents brought their children to Him, He would take them in His arms and bless them. Luke tells us that parents brought infants to Him just so He might touch them (Luke 18:15). Mark also speaks of a time when people brought little children to Jesus for His blessing. When the disciples protested, Jesus basically told them to back off. "Let the little children come to Me, and do not forbid them; for of such is the kingdom of God." He was never too busy to stop, gather a child into His arms, lay His hands on them and bless them (Mark 10:13-16).

In fact, just earlier Jesus had used a child to illustrate a point with His disciples on servanthood. As they were arguing over who would be the greatest among them, Jesus took a child into His arms and said, "Whoever receives one of these little children in My name receives Me; and whoever receives Me, receives not Me but Him who sent Me" (Mark 9:36-37). Can you imagine being held in His arms and hearing Him pronounce a blessing over you? I wonder how the lives of each of these children may have been changed or affected by His words. One can only imagine.

Each of us is to come to Jesus Christ as a child, with childlike faith. When we do, we become part of His family. Families take tea together. So every morning, I steep a cup of tea and open my Bible. I spend time with my Lord, reading, praying and listening. We spend time together, and He pours His blessing into my life. I want to do the same thing with the beautiful children God brings into my life. I never want to be too busy for them or turn them away. I do not have any of my own children, so each one that crosses my path is a gift.

The thought of physically being in the presence of Jesus in heaven and seeing Him face to face fills me with such excitement and anticipation, I feel like a little girl getting ready for her first tea party. I do hope there will be tea parties in heaven. And I hope I will be counted worthy to serve Him a cup of tea!

"Old" is a Good Thing

I have so many bags and tins of old tea on my shelf that are left over from the seven years I was a consultant for a home tea party business. After a few years, flavors fade and the tea tastes flat. Even using it to make iced tea ends with less than favorable results and they are relegated to the "round file."

So am I destined for the same fate as I grow older? Will I lose my flavor and be put on a back shelf somewhere to be considered of little value? It's been said that old age isn't for the timid. Our hair grays, our bones ache, and we move more slowly as we age. As part of the Baby Boomer generation, I have a lot of company as I gradually move into my senior years. Yet God's Word assures me that aging is not a bad thing.

I'd rather think of old age as a privilege, a blessing of being granted more years in this life. A dearly beloved uncle of mine died at the age of 51, and now I look back on that age as so young. God has given me many more years of life. My hair is slowly graying and my body is slowing down. Sometimes I look at growing older with trepidation, yet God's Word assures me that I need not fear. He will carry me into my old age and be my constant companion.

He tells me that He has upheld me and carried me from birth and "even to your old age and gray hairs I am He, I am He who will sustain you. I have made you and I will carry you; I will sustain you and I will rescue you" (Isaiah 46:3-4 NIV). Jesus is the Great Shepherd who "tends His flock…He gathers the lambs in His arms and carries them close to His heart" (Isaiah 40:11 NIV). So I do not need to fear growing old. God is with me all the way!

I've given up trying to count my gray hairs and now look at them as a badge of courage. After all, Solomon assures me in Proverbs 16:31 that "gray hair is a crown of splendor; it is attained by a righteous life." I will not cover those gray hairs with artificial color, but wear them proudly as my crown of splendor, a gift from the Lord. I will also seek ways to represent Him in this world; to remain useful in my old age and never lose my godly flavor in a world that is sometimes flat and tasteless; to continue to bear fruit for the Kingdom. As long as He carries me, I have value. He never throws away His own.

Lord, please help me to remember that You will carry me up to my last day on earth and then safely home to Heaven. Help me to not fear getting old and growing more vulnerable, but to take comfort in Your presence. May Your grace and mercy carry me through every day to come. Amen.

"Footprints"

One night I dreamed a dream.
I was walking along the beach with my Lord.
Across the dark sky flashed scenes from my life.
For each scene, I noticed two sets of footprints in the sand, one belonging to me and one to my Lord.
When the last scene of my life shot before me I looked back at the footprints in the sand.
There was only one set of footprints. I realized that this was at the lowest and saddest times of my life.
This always bothered me and I questioned the Lord about my dilemma.
"Lord, You told me when I decided to follow You, You would walk and talk with me all the way.
But I am aware that during the most troublesome times of my life there is only one set of footprints. I just don't understand why, when I needed You most, You leave me."
He whispered, "My precious child, I love you and will never leave you, never, ever, during your trials and testings. When you saw only one set of footprints it was then that I carried you."
- Anonymous

A Tea Hat or a Crown

The Queen has invited you to afternoon tea! This is a once-in-a-lifetime opportunity. Of course, you will want to look your best. You know she will be wearing a beautiful diamond-encrusted tiara or, if this is a formal affair, one of her golden crowns covered in priceless gems—probably one of the pieces housed under guard at the Tower of London with the rest of the Crown Jewels.

So what will you be wearing? A pretty afternoon tea hat is essential to be properly attired. It's a guarantee that the Queen will not be loaning you one of her tiaras or crowns. So you search your closet for the perfect outfit and matching hat, elegantly garnished with feathers, flowers, ribbons or even a few shiny baubles. If you have nothing suitable, off to the store you go. You cannot appear before the Queen without wearing a hat.

Crowns represent sovereignty. Kings and queens throughout history have worn crowns of precious metals and gems symbolizing their position, power and authority. In ancient Israel, King David wore a crown of gold befitting his high position (Psalm 21:3). Similarly, the High Priest wore a turban of white linen with a holy crown attached, a plate of pure gold engraved with the words "Holiness to the Lord." This crown signified the priest's authority and dedication to serve God in the Temple (Exodus 28:36-37; 29:6).

In Heaven, the King of Kings who wore a painful crown of thorns to the cross will be wearing a golden crown (Revelation 14:14). He will be surrounded in the Throne Room of Heaven by elders also wearing golden crowns which they cast at His feet as they worship Him. What will we be wearing when we stand before Him?

As believers in Jesus Christ, we are promised crowns to wear, not in this life, but in the next. Peter tells us in 1 Peter 5:4 that at His appearing, those who have faithfully shepherded the Church will receive crowns of glory that will not fade away. Paul teaches that those who serve Jesus in this life do so for the reward of an imperishable crown in the next (1 Corinthians 9:25). Those who faithfully serve Him and have loved His appearing are granted crowns of righteousness (2 Timothy 4:8). Those who have endured life's trials and have loved the Lord have been promised a crown of life from Him (James 1:12). Those who are faithful to Him through persecution until death will be given a crown of life by the Lord (Revelation 2:10). These crowns are part of the rewards promised to us in Heaven for our faith and service to our Lord during this earthly life.

When your afternoon tea with the Queen comes to an end, you are dismissed and your pretty tea hat is returned to the closet. You probably won't wear it again until the next tea party invitation comes along. In Heaven, our crowns are worn before the King of Kings. They are not kept under guard because of their value, but with the elders surrounding the Throne, we will cast them at the feet of Jesus, fall down before Him and say, "You are worthy, O Lord" (Revelation 4:10-11).

Which is more desirable to you? A stylish hat to wear to tea with the Queen or a precious crown with which to worship the King of Kings?

Dressed for Heaven

The hand of God formed Adam and Eve without clothing. They were naked and unashamed (Genesis 2:25). Every human being ever born since that day enters this world naked. It is a fact of life. No baby has ever appeared from his mother's womb wearing his first pair of onesies and booties. However, since the sin of Adam and Eve in the Garden of Eden, it is appropriate to be covered with clothing. To be naked in public for most of us would be shameful and humiliating.

On that note, let me share with you about the streaker who appeared at one of my tea parties! It is probably the most memorable moment in the seven years I hosted tea tastings. I was at a customer's home to serve her and her friends tea and scones and teach them about the proper preparation of loose leaf teas. All of the guests had already left. As I packed up my tea ware, her four-year-old daughter peeked around the corner from her bedroom, grinned and ran buck naked through the living room. Where was her pretty Disney princess dress? Apparently, this little one was the family streaker and didn't feel shame at being naked in front of a stranger. I am happy to say that I never had this happen again. But it's been fun to share the story.

Jesus encountered a streaker of sorts when He arrived by boat at the country of the Gadarenes on the Sea of Galilee. A naked man tormented by a legion of demons met Him at the shore. Luke tells the story of Jesus healing this poor soul who was living naked in the tombs and how He restored him to sanity. Citizens in the vicinity heard the story and came to find this man seated at the feet of Jesus, clothed and in his right mind (Luke 8:26-39 NIV). His humiliation and torment were over. He was a changed man.

Later, Jesus was to suffer His own humiliating circumstances at His crucifixion. It was a Roman custom to strip a person naked before they were crucified. Shame and humiliation were part of this method of execution. Jesus, who had committed no crime, probably suffered this punishment in addition to the nails in His feet and hands. Artists portray Him on the cross partially covered out of propriety, but He was most likely naked.

Jesus suffered the indignity of the cross naked and humiliated so that we could be clothed in robes of righteousness in Heaven. His broken body and shed blood prepared the way to make us acceptable to the Father by being clothed in His righteousness. Paul instructs us to put on Christ, that all of us who are baptized into Christ have clothed ourselves in Christ (Galatians 3:27 NIV). We have "put on" Christ as a garment (Romans 13:14 NIV).

The prophet Isaiah also speaks of garments. He tells us God has prepared a garment of praise instead of a spirit of despair. He will clothe us with garments of salvation and array us in robes of righteousness as brides and bridegrooms (Isaiah 61:3,10 NIV). At the Marriage Supper of the Lamb, when we celebrate the coming home of the Church to Heaven, we will be clothed in fine linens, clean and bright (Revelation 19:8 NIV).

We were born naked. All our sins are exposed and laid bare before our Holy God (Hebrews 4:13). But if we are children of God clothed in the righteousness of Jesus Christ, we will be properly dressed for Heaven. There will be no more shame, and we will be dressed in the glory of our Lord. What a beautiful day that will be!

Seated at His Table

I don't know about you, but I feel honored both to prepare a tea table for friends and to be invited to someone else's tea table. Both bring me joy. I spend a lot of time focused on planning the table decorations, because that is the first thing people see when they enter the room—a colorful table with just the right linens, china patterns, and flowers to tie it all together and welcome my guests. I also look forward to seeing how others dress their tea tables. This creates the first impression of "welcome to my home."

Next comes an array of scones, cream and lemon curd; assorted savory sandwiches; bite-sized sweets; and, of course, pot after pot of aromatic teas. There is much work and time involved in planning, decorating and preparing food for a proper afternoon tea, yet it is always done in love, desiring that everyone at the table feels special and blessed.

Scripture tells us that Jesus sat at the tables of disciples, Pharisees, sinners and friends during His ministry on earth. What was served wasn't important to Him, but the conversation and the people He spent His time with were extremely important to Him. Much of His teaching was done at these tables, and all who would listen were blessed.

Jesus had His final meal on earth with His beloved disciples at the Last Supper of Passover. The table was prepared, and they all gathered around it to share bread and wine with the Lord (Matthew 26:26-29). Today we celebrate at the "communion table" by taking bread and wine to represent the Lord's sacrifice for us on the cross. We remember His death, resurrection and the New Covenant Jesus instituted for the forgiveness of sins by His shed blood.

David praised God in Psalm 23:5 because He "prepares a table before me in the presence of my enemies." God provides for our needs at an earthly table. One day those of us who have believed and been adopted into the family of God will all be invited to Jesus's table in heaven to the Marriage Supper of the Lamb (Revelation 19:9). I wonder what will be on the menu at this great celebration. At my tea table, I always serve scones and tea. Jesus usually had bread and wine at His meals. He told His disciples at their last meal with Him that He wouldn't drink wine again until He drinks it with His children in His Father's kingdom (Matthew 26:29). So I imagine there will be bread and wine at His table in heaven.

What is served is not as important as the privilege to be seated at the Marriage Supper of the Lamb with other brothers and sisters in Christ. Those at His table will feel special and blessed beyond measure, whatever is served. You will only be invited to this table if you have embraced Jesus as Lord and Savior and all He did for you on the cross. Could be He is even preparing this table for us as you are reading these words. Will I see you there?

What Will You Choose Today?

Choices. There are so many choices to make every day. What will I wear today? What shall I have for breakfast? Which route will I take to work? What will I watch on TV? What book shall I read? And on it goes. Every morning I stand at the kitchen counter asking myself, "Which tea do I feel like drinking this morning?" Breakfast Black? Assam? Irish Cream? There are so many choices, but this should be a relatively simple one to make.

There are many other choices that are more difficult for me, the most important one being, what will I do with Jesus today? If He is truly Lord of my life, then this is one of the most important choices I can make. Will I serve "self" or "Savior?" Will I lead or follow? Will I give or receive? Will I deny myself or indulge myself? Will I serve or be served? Will I worry or trust Him today? What will I choose at any given moment throughout the day?

When I take time to think about all the choices He made for me, from leaving the throne room of Heaven all the way to suffering the agony of the cross—for ME—the answers to my questions become clear. I must choose Jesus. What tea I drink every morning won't greatly affect my day, but choosing to follow Jesus each morning determines the course of the day and my life. Knowing that I am prone to selfishness, I can only strive to make the godly choice at every opportunity and trust His Spirit to lead me.

With that first cup of tea in the morning, I choose to sit with my Lord and His Word. To fill my mind and heart with the words of Scripture and allow God to speak to me is the best choice I can make to start a new day. I do not claim to always be the most graceful and obedient follower, but that is the intent of my heart. I love my Lord, and I love His Word. What better way to prepare for today than to spend some quiet time with Him over a cuppa and my Bible! That is the best choice I can make for every new morning He gives me.

"Choose for yourselves this day whom you will serve" (Joshua 24:15a).

What or whom will *you* choose today?

Lord, please help me make good choices today that please You. Guide me in the path you would have me take. Amen.

Photo by freestocks.org from Pexels

Are You Ready?

Being prepared is very important to me. After all, I was a Brownie when I was a little girl. The Girl Scout motto is "Be prepared." If I'm planning a tea party, I spend a lot of time cleaning house, planning the menu, grocery shopping, decorating the table, and preparing food. My goal is to have hot tea on the table and all the food ready to serve when my first guest arrives. I want to be free to visit with them and focus on my guests rather than my tea sandwiches. This takes careful planning ahead and well-timed preparation.

I recall one tea tasting event I did several years ago. I arrived an hour before the party was to begin. Instead of finding my hostess ready for me, everything was in a state of unreadiness. She was in the process of vacuuming carpets and mopping floors. She frantically set up her tables and chairs. As guests began to arrive, I was asked to unpack and wash a large box of teacups. No cups had been prepared. As I washed, she finished getting dressed and then enlisted me to zip up her dress. This hostess was definitely unprepared. Much was left until the last minute which caused us both unnecessary stress.

What stands out to me most about this event was the state of unreadiness. It reminds me of the parable of the ten virgins in Matthew 25:1-13. Ten virgins are waiting for the bridegroom's procession to arrive, and they take their lamps to light the way as they wait. Five wise virgins take oil for their lamps, and five foolish virgins take no oil. As the bridegroom is delayed, they all fall asleep. When the wedding procession is on its way, five lamps are lit, while the others remain dark. Since there isn't enough oil for everyone, the unprepared virgins go off to buy some. While they are gone, the bridegroom arrives, and the five wise virgins are off to the wedding celebration while the others find the door shut when they return. When they ask to be let in, the answer they receive is, "I do not know you."

Jesus shares this parable to make the point that we need to be prepared for His second coming. "Watch therefore, for you know neither the day nor the hour in which the Son of Man is coming" (v.13). Jesus, who is our Bridegroom, promised that after He left this earth, He would return again. As the wise virgins prepared themselves with lamps and oil to meet the Bridegroom, so we need to be prepared for that day we will meet the Lord. We don't want to hear Him say, "I do not know you." So how can we be prepared? Will we be ready when He comes? What does that look like?

- ❖ <u>Have you received an invitation?</u> God extends an invitation to relationship with Himself to every person through His Son, Jesus Christ. He …"desires all men to be saved and to come to the knowledge of the truth" (1 Timothy 2:4).

- ❖ <u>Have you accepted the invitation?</u> By accepting, we welcome Jesus into our lives, are born again, and receive eternal life with Him (John 3:16). God invites, but our part is to accept.

- ❖ <u>Do you know the Bridegroom?</u> A wedding ceremony just isn't as meaningful when you don't know either the bride or the groom. Peter encourages us to "grow in the grace and knowledge of our Lord and Savior Jesus Christ" (2 Peter 3:18). I want to be able to say with Paul that "I know whom I have believed" (2 Timothy 1:12) and that I will recognize Him when He comes.

- ❖ <u>Are you on His guest list?</u> Is your name written in God's Book of Life? "Only those who are written in the Lamb's Book of Life" will be admitted into heaven (Revelation 21:27). If you have received Jesus into your life, you are on the list. He knows those who are His (John 10:14).

- ❖ <u>Is your lamp lit?</u> The prophet Samuel declares, "For You are my lamp, O Lord" (2 Samuel 22:29). Not only is He our lamp, but He is our light (Psalm 18:28). Jesus is the light of the world (John 8:12). His light is found in His Word, the Bible: "a lamp to my feet and a light to my path" (Psalm 119:105). Reading and studying the Bible to know God better is a great joy and privilege.

- ❖ <u>Are you watching and waiting for Him?</u> I pray for an expectant heart that will rejoice when I see His face. I invite you to stand with me as one of those "looking for the blessed hope and glorious appearing of our great God and Savior Jesus Christ" (Titus 2:13).

We do not know when He will come. So if you want to be ready and not be left out of the celebration on that day, I encourage you to prepare yourselves. Accept God's invitation, get to know Jesus, make sure you're on His guest list, and be waiting expectantly for His arrival. It will be a moment of great joy and celebration!

Notes

1. Souter, K. (2013). *The Tea Cyclopedia*. New York, NY: Skyhorse Publishing, pages 4-6

2. Arthur, Kay. (1992). *Lord, I Want to Know You*. Portland, OR: Multnomah Press

3. Alleyne, R. (2009, August) A Cup of tea really can help reduce stress at times of crisis, claim scientists. *The Telegraph*. Retrieved from http://www.telegraph.co.uk/news/science/science-news/6015821/A-cup-of-tea-really-can-help-reduce-stress-at-times-of-crisis-claim-scientists.html

Made in the USA
Monee, IL
16 August 2023